PRAISE FOR
HOODOO JUSTICE MAGIC

T0109545

"*Hoodoo Justice Magic* by Miss Aida is a treasure trove of information, psalms, herbs, and curios all designed to obtain justice for the disenfranchised, downtrodden, and defenseless. Well written with a practiced hand and a caring voice, this book empowers those experiencing issues in love, the workplace, and even friend groups. A must-have!"

> —AMY BLACKTHORN, founder of Blackthorn's Botanicals and author of *Blackthorn's Botanical Magic*

""What a deviously delicious book, written with Miss Aida's expertise and wit. Witches and Hoodoo folk can pick up a few new tricks. *Hoodoo Justice Magic* is a must for your spell-working library."

> —JOANIE MARIE, founder of the Pagan and Witch Proud Facebook group

"I was very excited to read Miss Aida's new book, *Hoodoo Justice Magic,* and I absolutely love it! There is some old school, heavy-hitting stuff in this book that reminds me of how the "backwoods" root workers would settle a score—justifiably! As a palera and a root worker, I highly recommend *Hoodoo Justice Magic* to every practitioner."

> —LELIA MARINO, Yaya Nkisi, proprietress of Ms. Rain's Conjure Shop, and creator of the *Real Life Oracle*

"I love *Hoodoo Justice Magic;* I can't put it down! It feels like more than just a book. It feels as if Miss Aida is physically present in the room with the reader. Her energy—simultaneously strong and nurturing—breathes life into every word. I can hear her voice in my head and feel her hands on my hands, guiding, counseling, teaching, and supporting me in righteous vindication every step of the way."

—MARY-GRACE FAHRUN, author of *Italian Folk Magic*

"*Hoodoo Justice Magic* is a work that has been carefully crafted to get to the very heart of a modern-day worker's intentions. There are many titles that line countless shelves that purport to be tried and true sources of ancestral wisdom. Unfortunately, not many have stood the test of time. Fortunately for us, Miss Aida has compiled a thorough catalogue of spells that target many specific needs in our hectic, everyday lives. From having an ethical reason to engage in the work to the spell itself, through all the possibilities of its success or failure, *Hoodoo Justice Magic* will aid you every step of the way. Miss Aida has shared with us the wisdom of her own ancestors. This book is true enlightenment and needs to be in every Hoodoo and magical worker's library."

—TIM SHAW, host of the Black Cat Lounge and author of *Ghosts of Buffalo*

"Sometimes we feel powerless to prevent injustice and are told never to take justice into our own hands, but that doesn't apply to all situations. There are times when we need to use Magical Justice to regain our power, protect ourselves or our loved ones, and settle the score. In her infinite wisdom, Miss Aida has conjured up the ideal spell book to do just that. Whether it's a hex, a curse, or a need to get the upper hand in a pesky situation, *Hoodoo Justice Magic* is a treasure trove of spells that will enable the reader to right the wrongs in a hands-on and straightforward way."

—MARLA BROOKS, author of *Workplace Spells* and *Animal Spells and Magick*

"Fear not. The scales of justice have just weighed in your favor and righteous protection is a mere page away. Everything you need can be found in the pages of *Hoodoo Justice Magic*, a complete guide to protecting yourself, getting justice, or, if you prefer, payback. Miss Aida covers it all—the good, the bad, the ugly, as well as the ethics of retribution. A must-have in everyone's collection, *Hoodoo Justice Magic* offers empowerment via a magical education."

—BRYAN M. BOWDEN, founder and director
of the New York State UFO Project

"As always, Miss Aida stands out as an author in the field of Hoodoo both for her vast understanding of the subject and her generous way of explaining each concept and each principle in simple terms, not leaving out any detail. *Hoodoo Justice Magic* is the perfect guide to inspire and teach you how to take justice into your own hands when warranted, speed up legal processes and turn them to your advantage, resolve ambiguous situations, and learn to protect yourself and find divine guidance in the process."

—ELHOIM LEAFAR, author of *The Magical
Art of Crafting Charm Bags* and *Manifestation Magic*

HOODOO
JUSTICE
MAGIC

HOODOO
JUSTICE
MAGIC

Spells for Power, Protection and Righteous Vindication

MISS AIDA

WEISER BOOKS

This edition first published in 2021 by Weiser Books, an imprint of
Red Wheel/Weiser, LLC
With offices at:
65 Parker Street, Suite 7
Newburyport, MA 01950
www.redwheelweiser.com

Copyright © 2021 by Kerrjie Aida Severini, MS, BSN, RN

ISBN: 978-1-57863-756-0
Library of Congress Cataloging-in-Publication Data available upon
request.

Cover design by Kathryn Sky-Peck
Tarot card image derived from the Waite deck created by Red Wheel/
    Weiser, LLC.
Interior by Happenstance Type-O-Rama
Typeset in Walbaum, Dress, and Above the Sky

Printed in the United States of America
IBI

10 9 8 7 6 5 4 3 2 1

This book is dedicated in loving
memory to my parents
Nick Catel and Kiriaki Catel

CONTENTS

ACKNOWLEDGMENTS

How about this badass book cover? Upon seeing it for the first time, my mouth dropped wide open, and I was rendered speechless. This masterpiece was conceived by Weiser's creative director, Kathryn Sky-Peck, who also designed the book cover for my last book *Hoodoo Cleansing and Protection Magic*. Thank you, Kathryn!

I've met some phenomenal people on this journey as an author, especially at Weiser publishing company. Peter Turner, Jane Hagaman, Greg Brandenburgh, Eryn Eaton, Michelle Spanedda, and, of course, Judika Illes. I don't want to forget the very nice Sylvia Hopkins because she's the lady who pays me! A special gratitude is extended to Ashley Benning, the copyeditor for both of my books published by Weiser. Being a copyeditor, in my humble opinion, is a tough job—especially having to deal with me and my somewhat obsessive ways!

My friends who follow me on Facebook know that this year I lost Wolfie, one of my German Shepherd dogs. He was the sunshine of my life and is missed terribly by me and my other two fur-babies, Asha and Junior. So I wanted to take this opportunity to pay tribute to him.

We love and miss you, Wolfie. Rest in Peace my *beautiful* little boy.

Athena's Wolfgang vom Atlas
October 2, 2009–January 20, 2021

PREFACE
What Is Hoodoo?

Hoodoo—also known as Conjure, tricking, or rootwork—is a form of folk magic practiced in North America. It incorporates Central and West African magic along with integrated fragments of Jewish, Christian, Irish, German, Spanish, Asian, and Native American beliefs and practices.

For many decades, the secrets of Hoodoo were passed down to successive generations solely through oral traditions. But since that time, famous people, such as anthropologist and author Zora Neale Hurston (1891–1960), have written books about Hoodoo practices that remain available today. Its popularity increased when, in the 1930s, the Reverend Harry Middleton Hyatt began gathering folkloric information from more than 1,600 sources, from here on in to be called "the Hyatt informants." These people were predominantly the descendants of enslaved Africans, who resided throughout the southern United States. Hyatt subsequently published a five-volume, 4,766-page collection entitled *Hoodoo—Conjuration—Witchcraft—Rootwork* (HCWR).

But even while these written compilations were going out into the world, thousands of practitioners were not sharing their secrets so widely, but continued to pass down their knowledge in the oral tradition to their families. These successors, in turn, passed what they knew down to their descendants and confidants. So this is not a kind of magic found only in reference books and stories of the past. It is an ongoing living tradition.

In recent decades, numerous books have been written on the topic of Hoodoo. Educational classes are offered that greatly appeal to the general public—most likely because of the beauty of its simplicity and its effectiveness. But not one person has all the answers or a single "correct" way of performing Hoodoo magic, because oral traditions have pioneered the enriching variations of this wondrous craft that continue to this day.

INTRODUCTION

Justice is the moral principle that is supposed to determine rightful conduct and the administration of deserved punishment for wrong actions or reward for right ones. When people meet with injustices, such as unfair treatment or undeserved outcomes, they expect their friends, loved ones, family, neighbors, coworkers, superiors, and most especially the legal system to understand what just conduct looks like and to immediately support them in their predicament. Sadly, victims can instead be met with apathy, or sometimes even active blame-placing.

Where does this leave a victim of injustice who has lost social standing, a significant other, or a job promotion duly earned to an undeserving predator? What happens to those facing harassment, prejudice, bullying, and threats instead of a balancing of the scales? What does one do when the legal system fails a victim of physical violence, robbery, theft, or other crimes? When the processes society has put in place don't work as they should, a person could easily succumb to feelings of desperation, despair, helplessness, and/or hopelessness. Or that victim can take a route that has been used for thousands of years—magical retribution!

Magical Justice—Past and Present

Our ancestors fell victim to injustices as do people today. They too were double-crossed and betrayed and were the target of crimes. When they did not receive the justice they deserved from society, they sought their retribution though magical incantations, spellwork, and/or prayers instead. Their accounts, as well as their formulas, have been well-documented throughout recorded history and from around the world.

In his book *The Encyclopedia of Jewish Myth, Magic and Mysticism*, Rabbi Geoffrey Dennis writes that humans have the power to curse individuals as well as groups of people. He states that Psalms 35, 58, and 137 "invoke hair raising afflictions"; however, Psalm 109 is the most powerful text for retribution. Historians estimate that Psalm 109—to be provided later in this book—was written in the year 1060 BC. So we can see that magic has worked for thousands of years—and can work for you too! The proof of magical paybacks is right in our very own Holy Bible.

This book will provide numerous spells intended to serve out justice to those who have violated the principles of morality—just as our ancestors prevailed over their enemies.

Spells are provided to send enemies away, bind them from doing or saying harmful things, break up a relationship when a partner was taken away from you, and—harshest of all—curse/cross/hex. And once these are accomplished, they can result in the restoration of both self-respect and respect from others—things which every single human being is entitled to.

But first, let's examine the types of enemies you can encounter—because the more you know about their tactics, the better prepared you are to counter them.

Intentional Wrongdoers Are Immoral

Morals relate to the standards of good intentions and honesty, as well as fair and equal interactions with and treatment of everyone. Morals speak to defining the principles of right and wrong behaviors. People who abide by these standards are referred to as moral or righteous.

Values, on the other hand, talk about what people believe to be true and hold in high esteem. They are the factors that influence the choices made by each individual and generate types of behavior. Most people value the morals of righteousness they were taught at an early age, and therefore, they conduct themselves accordingly. They are decent people who have worked hard to achieve their goals.

Sadly, not everyone is guided by moral principles but instead may value power, status, wealth, notoriety, and/or gratifying their desires. These people believe they are entitled to whatever they wish without having to work for it, and they can and will act out that belief at any cost and without regard for others. They are immoral people. Most, if not all, are predators such as narcissists, sociopaths, con artists, scammers, or abusers who are looking for prey in hopes of stealing something of value. They are lazy people motivated by greed, jealousy, envy, and/or a sense of entitlement, and they accomplish their goals with whatever tactics they can.

Immoral Tactics

* *Deception* is common for fraudulent people who will try lying, labeling, scapegoating, false accusations, blame-placing, and demeaning others or their work ethics to get what they want. These people wish to rob others of their positions, social status, significant others, material possessions, and even identities.

* *Emotional abuse* is a frequent tool they use for self-empowerment. They may look for targets whose weaknesses are transparent. Then they dominate their victims by instilling fear or suppressing their self-esteem through harassment, threats, or working to change other people's regard for them.

* *Physical abuse* is usually, but not always, inflicted by those who had been constantly belittled and thus

developed poor self-esteem along with a habit of venting their own negative emotions through aggression. They are often bullies seeking to act out their anger toward others who are vulnerable and unable to defend themselves. Their victims are usually smaller in stature and/or are viewed as having a physical or emotional weakness. People who resort to emotional abuse will often dish out physical abuse as well.

* *Theft* is taking something away from a victim without their knowledge. Examples could include someone having a secret affair with your significant other or getting you demoted at work or even dismissed, while this person replaces you without any justifiable cause.

* *Robbery,* on the other hand, is when someone takes from you by force or threat. This could include an eviction without cause, blackmail, filing false police reports or court actions against you to force some desired action, or taking ownership of something you value.

How Do Wrongdoers Get Away with All This and What Can You Do?

All these tactics of immoral people are reprehensible, and many are also illegal. Why do so many who use them escape punishment? They know the loopholes, are cunning about how they operate, and stay alert and aware of their surroundings and any potential threats to their activities.

If you are faced with one of these immorals and they have managed to harm you without anyone spotting them, there are ways to get back your own. This book provides an arsenal of spells to obtain your well-deserved justice.

Always keep in mind that magical justice must be secret and hidden. Would a military general broadcast a planned sneak attack during a war? Of course not, because the enemies would be able to prepare a defense. This comparison to the military goes further, though: please remember, this artillery of magical spells can be dangerous; therefore, you must treat them with caution, just as you would a loaded rifle. And the main way you do this is by looking at your situation with clear eyes to know when magical justice can be safely used. You must be *justified* to perform these spells. Otherwise, you will be as culpable as your rivals. . . . Are you justified? We'll explore the concept of justification in chapter 1.

What's Your Strategy?

Before attempting negative spellwork, it is essential to first have a game plan. During wartime when soldiers prepare to engage their enemies, they just don't haphazardly begin attacking. First, they consider if an attack is vindicated. If it is, they know that they must calmly formulate a strategy because if they acted solely from emotion and without a plan, their attack would most likely go awry and lead to disastrous results. Once they have carefully scrutinized the type of attacks, they factor in timing as well as consider which allies will assist them before they put their plan into action. In other words, successful attacks must be executed in a well-thought-out manner. The planning phase is vital for any type of effective combat—and that includes spiritual confrontations. Without a strategy, bad results will most likely prevail. This chapter addresses how to set up successful strategies before taking any action.

Step 1. Your Spellwork Must Be Justified

When people are offended, emotionally wounded, or mistreated, it provokes their anger—the intense emotion that triggers the body's fight-or-flight response. Once this reflex is set off, an accelerated physiological response is put in motion that, in turn, bypasses rational thinking and prepares the body for immediate action. If you are a person who tends to fight rather than flee, just remember that most situations triggering this response are not life-threatening. Try to remove yourself from the setting because any reaction you have in the heat of anger could compromise your safety and bring on legal ramifications. Seek your vengeance through the proper legal channels and, if that doesn't work, through spellwork.

However, when utilizing spellcraft, always remember that justice is the administering of a *deserved* punishment or reward. Most importantly, justice is also based on the principle that the punishment should be proportionate to the offense.

This isn't something to take up just because your feelings are hurt or you aren't getting everything you always wanted but with good reason. Take your emotions out of it, and look clearly at what is going on: Is the situation you want to correct all about you? That's a red flag that you are still caught up in anger. Or is it instead a situation where someone is behaving immorally and getting a free pass? Should society be correcting this action but just isn't? Will your community—and not just you and your feelings—be better off once consequences are imposed?

I deal with some pretty vulgar people on a routine basis and sometimes, in fleeting thoughts, I consider harsh magical revenge. But I also know that spellwork is a very serious matter, and severe harm could be inflicted without proper justification. Therefore, my policy is to wait about a week to reassess feelings toward the person who has offended me. After time passes, usually, my anger will have subsided, and I am grateful that my time, energy, or money for supplies weren't wasted.

Remember that when people are angry or enraged, our thought processes can get distorted. If negative spellwork is performed while in that state of mind, dire consequences could manifest. You could impose serious harm out of proportion to the situation because, with all that fast-tracked energy being emitted, a spell can go way beyond your initial intentions.

Spells Don't Backfire. But . . .

Novice spellcasters will frequently hastily plan to retaliate when someone makes them angry by bestowing ongoing bad luck on their *target*—the intended object of a spell. However, rage results in unclear thinking and this can lead to spellwork that manifests as permanent debilitating physiological damage, horrific automobile and motorcycle accidents, or loss of limbs. In three cases that I am aware of, enraged spellcasting has led to death—all because the caster was not of clear mind and didn't think things through. These punishments were neither fair to the targets nor justified. Karmic paybacks can be brutal and, unless those casters sincerely repent of their actions, somewhere or somehow, those targets will be avenged.

Karmic payback multiplies for unjustified negative spells. I once knew a woman who presumptuously professed she would curse anyone she pleased and believed that karmic payback was a bunch of nonsense. She suffered from ongoing bad luck with her financial matters, her romantic pursuits, and her son's upbringing and frequently experienced suicidal ideations. Then she would perpetually call me and ask: "Why do all these bad things only happen to me?" Well, those unjustified curses had an impact.

You don't send someone away, bind them, or curse them just because that person annoys you, is unattractive, doesn't agree with your philosophical or political views, or out of prejudice. People should be sent away or bound when they pose some sort of threat to you. Breakup spells should only be performed in situations when someone has stolen your significant other or if the breakup will save one party from present or future harm. And cursing spells are reserved only for retaliation for the most horrific assaults to you or your loved ones.

Always remember what God said in the Holy Bible, Exodus 21:24–25 (KJV):

Eye for eye, tooth for tooth, hand for hand, foot for foot,

Burning for burning, wound for wound, stripe for stripe.

In other words, the punishment must be proportionate to the crime. So before performing negative spells, calm down and think about the entire situation to ensure you have a just cause for what you plan to do and you are only taking an eye for an eye and not pushing for more.

Step 2. Adjust Your Attitude

Your mind-set must be properly conditioned for any type of successful spellcasting. Although the conditioning isn't difficult, it does require four fundamentals for victorious outcomes:

* **Self-confidence:** You must be self-confident that your spells will work. This means that you ought not second-guess yourself or fear you are not powerful enough to control the target. With self-confidence, you also have to be determined to affect the target and to be patient with your work.

* **Determination:** While performing magic, some spell-casters will monitor their target and get dismayed when that target is doing well. Rather than realizing that social media can be deceptive, they then lose confidence and surrender their spellwork while assuming nothing is manifesting. This is the wrong attitude. The correct

approach is to continue your work. Be determined to see it through to manifestation without a change of heart.

* **Patience:** This is a virtue that is absolutely necessary because spells don't work overnight! No matter what happens, be calm and know that your dedication will pay off!

* **Persistence:** Repeat the spells, add more spells (for a cumulative effect), or try different ones, as needed.

A True Inspirational Story

This story posted on my website, MissAida.com, illustrates exactly what I am talking about:

The following true and astonishing success story of a justified curse will illustrate how the four essential fundamentals of self-confidence, determination, patience, and persistence are implemented.

Decades ago, there was a man named Tony, a happily married and successful spiritual practitioner and owner of a flourishing spiritual store. He was a *babalawo*, a powerful and high-ranking priest in the religion of Santería. He also had a successful house of Santería, called an *ile*, with numerous members who loved and admired him. Because of his popularity and charm, people traveled long distances to seek his services.

My Godmother in Santería also adored Tony, as did I, and had practically worked her fingers to the bone for many months assisting him with his numerous ceremonies. She also happily contributed her vast years of wisdom and knowledge in any way that she could; however, her services also required payments. She had desperately depended on money to pay for her family members' departure from the impoverished country of Cuba to the United States, what she called "the country of freedom."

Unfortunately, wealth and notoriety got the best of the babalawo, and he transformed from a thoughtful man to a greedy "green-eyed monster." He was keeping all of the profits to himself while perpetually stalling to pay my Godmother for her services. Ultimately, he never paid her one single penny and cheated her out of thousands of dollars.

But my Godmother wasn't an idiot, either. On every single visit to Tony's home or store, she collected his stray hair and other personal concerns (to be discussed later in this book), professing that these items might be needed for a "rainy day." Sadly, that "rainy day" arrived when she came to the realization that Tony had no intention of ever paying her. So with these personal concerns, she made a doll in his image.

In her backyard, the doll-baby was hanging by its neck, tied to a tree branch. I asked: "Godmother, who is this?" She angrily replied: "It's Tony. When I am finished with him, he will lose his wife, his house, his business, and his savings. I will destroy him just the way he destroyed my children and my grandchildren!" Truthfully, I thought to myself that the old lady was crazy to think that a mere *santera*, such as herself, could ruin such a powerful spiritual practitioner. But she was confident that she would destroy him. So, every single day, day after day, she would tirelessly beat the crap out of that doll with a heavy stick while demanding that he lose his wife, house, business, and money. My Godmother was determined to ruin Tony's life.

Two months later, she was still cursing the doll. Honestly, it was exhausting me just to watch her constantly beating and yelling at it! Being impetuously outspoken, I had the stupidity to question her actions: "Madrina, you're wasting your time. The spell is not working. Nothing is going to happen to Tony. As a matter of fact, his business is flourishing and he's thinking of expanding his store." With disgust and contempt toward my confrontation she replied: "You have no faith! You have no patience, and that lack of patience will destroy your spells and your life!" Several weeks later, she was still beating that doll with that heavy stick while screaming her demands. She was a persistent spellcaster with no intentions of giving up, even with all of Tony's blatant ongoing successes.

A couple of months after my Godmother had scolded me, I received a phone call from Maria, the babalawo's wife. She wanted to inform me that she had caught Tony making love to another woman in her very own bed! I immediately informed my Godmother and her response was: "Good. Now, sit back and enjoy the show because it's just beginning." From that moment forward, Tony's life started falling apart. And the "show" was indeed just beginning!

Because the Santería community holds babalawos to a higher ethical and moral standard, adultery is not tolerated. So as retaliation for the hurt that Maria suffered, she had called every member of his ile, and as many of his clients, friends, and followers as she could to expose his disregard of the religious standards. Maria was determined to destroy his reputation.

Next, Maria withdrew all the money from his bank accounts, moved away, and then filed for divorce. The courts awarded her a large sum of money in lieu of the physical home and business. After Maria ruined Tony's reputation as a virtuous man, he was left with a failed business and no money to pay the mortgage. He lost his followers, his home, and his business.

The manifestation of my Godmother's spellwork resulted in a fast deterioration of everything that Tony had worked so hard to attain. As a matter of fact, it took only about a year to destroy what Tony had worked decades to build. It was also amazing to watch Tony's very own wife be the catalyst for the curse. The spiritual entities working alongside my Godmother used the best possible means to manifest her goals.

Was my Godmother's spell of revenge justified? Of course it was! Tony's greed and lack of payments kept her children and grandchildren impoverished. So she did the same to him. The punishment was clearly proportionate to the offense.

By the way, Tony feverishly attempted to rebuild the empire he once had but was unsuccessful. Later, he disappeared. To this day, nobody seems to know where he is or what happened to him. He just seemed to have perished.

What were the lesson to be learned? My Godmother's self-confidence, determination, patience, and persistence caused the justifiable destruction to the life of a very powerful man. She was a master of her craft!

Step 3. Honor the Golden Rule: Keep Quiet!

Never tell your friends that you plan to, or are, performing negative spellwork. This is self-sabotaging and a recipe for failure, because if a trusted friend inadvertently reveals your secret to others, the communication channels may lead back to your enemies. Once they learn of your plans, it allows them an opportunity to protect themselves. Even if they don't believe in magic, in most circumstances they will don amulets or other protective gear just to be safe. Remember the old saying: "Loose lips sink ships."

If an enemy is also a spiritual practitioner, that person will go to extreme measures to boost their protection techniques. The solution is to patiently wait until the person believes that extra protection is no longer needed and feels comfortable enough to abandon the measures. In other words, wait until their guard is down.

Yes, sometimes it may take time to seek your justice, but it's better to wait than to engage in unproductive practices. That's easier said than done, but patience is indeed a virtue.

Additionally, never carelessly expose your spellwork to others. It causes curiosity, intrigue, and, ultimately, gossip. Keep your spellwork hidden at all times!

Step 4. Select the Proper Spells to Avoid Future Problems

When engaging in spiritual warfare, always consider the innocent bystanders who may be in the direct "line of fire" and the possible consequences of your attack plans. When you carefully consider the consequences and potential casualties of negative spellwork in your planning phase, it is easier to change the spell type to avoid the ramifications before they happen, rather than having to repair them after the fact.

Numerous clients have told me stories of innocent people being injured as a result of their negative spellwork. They usually profess that "the spell backfired," which is an inaccurate assumption. Spells do not backfire—but sometimes it is simply that outcomes go awry as a result of insufficient planning. I'll share with you of one of the many mistakes I personally made from acting impetuously as an example.

Many years ago, I had a neighbor named Susan who disapproved of my nationality. She continuously engaged in gossip and slander against me with another neighbor named Abbey. One day, after Susan saw me on the porch with a skull candle, she became overly emotional and this led both her and Abbey to treat me with overt antagonism. Without thoughtful planning, I hastily performed move away spells—rather than a stop gossip spell—on Susan, believing that the gossip and slander would cease if she were gone. The spell was successful as she moved away, but unfortunately, she sold her house to a mentally unstable man.

This man, in turn, immediately developed a friendship with Abbey, and the cycle of vicious gossip, slander, and intrigue against me resumed and even intensified. Because he was not of sound mind, he perpetually harassed and threatened me—a woman twenty years his senior and half his size—as an attempt to force *me* to move away. Abbey was frequently there to cheer him on. Fearing for my life, I had to take legal action against him as well as performing binding and cursing spells on both him and Abbey.

That was a lot of unnecessary damage control because I didn't consider the consequences of chasing Susan away nor did I factor in the possibility that Abbey was the actual ringleader in the campaign against me. It was a powerful learning event for which I am grateful, because our many mistakes bring us to experience and wisdom!

To prevent the harming of innocent people or producing an undesired aftermath—such as the one I experienced—do not select a negative spell on impulse. Instead, do so calmly and in a thoughtful and calculated manner:

1. Select several spells that are appealing to you.

2. Document the purpose of each spell. Then, under each spell listed . . .

3. Consider the short-term and long-term rewards of each spell if it is manifested.

4. Consider the short-term and long-term consequences of each spell if it is manifested.

5. Ensure that the spells will not hurt innocent people as a side effect if your target is debilitated.

6. Eliminate the spells that may produce unwanted consequences.

7. Through the process of elimination, choose the spells that you believe will yield the best outcomes.

Why Select More Than One Spell to Perform?

All living beings and matter possess auras, which are radiant energy fields that act as shields that protect us from outside negative influences that might affect our psychological and spiritual well-being. A healthy and radiant aura will easily ward off undesirable forces and sustain optimal living conditions.

Since the objective of negative spellwork is to penetrate the target's aura in order to impose your will upon their present emotional or physiological condition, this will be easier to do if the enemy's aura has already been damaged from negative events such as a psychological, physiological, or spiritual illness. Such negative events can cause a suppression, tears, or holes in the aura, making it easier to get through.

However, if an aura is healthy and radiant, it will most likely take more than one spell, or spiritual event, for your spell to be realized. This can be compared to piling straws on a camel's back. Eventually, the camel will have accumulated too much weight, which will eventually break its back.

Always Be Conscientious about Fire Safety

When working with incense, candles, or any type of flames or fires, always be diligent regarding their placement to prevent a conflagration. Never place anything combustible near them. Unless otherwise directed, incense ought to be placed only on a censer, while candles are set in a candleholder. Then I personally put my candleholders on a metal container, such as a pie plate that sits over two stacked cork coasters. Other practitioners scatter sand on the altar for their censers or candleholders to sit on top of.

Step 5. Scrutinize Your Verbal and Written Requests

A verbal request or command is a *petition*, and if it is written on a piece of paper to be used in ritual, it is called a *petition paper*. Both must be carefully analyzed before implementing spellwork, because they hold a tremendous amount of power.

The old adage of "Be careful what you wish for, you may receive it" is a powerful warning that must be respected and heeded in spellwork. When people state their desires verbally, they are releasing sound, and that sound disperses as energy, which is emitted into the spirit world as well as into the universe. If that energy is distributed correctly, someone or something is bound to honor the request. Therefore, it is essential to compose your petition in a clear and concise manner while again considering the consequences of powerful words.

Written requests are equally as powerful as verbal ones. When a petition paper is incorporated into spellwork, it becomes an ingredient and will be acknowledged by the spirit world.

In both instances, your words must be carefully chosen to avoid unintended future consequences. One of the most common mistakes neophyte practitioners make is setting the stage for an undesirable aftermath by misusing open-ended statements. Examples to avoid include:

* **The target will suffer.** Consider how *suffering* will be interpreted by the target and not by you, the spellcaster. Suffering might manifest as the death of an innocent loved one, such as a child, a parent, a significant other, or a pet.

* **The couple will suffer together and break up.** Again, you don't know what the catalyst for suffering might be for that couple. The loss of a child? One person being debilitated for life and in need of constant medical care?

* **The target will be miserable.** As with the word *suffer*, *misery* may also involve an innocent bystander who is associated with the target becoming a casualty.

* **The target will endure pain.** How will this pain be manifested? Is this emotional or physical pain that you wish for them? Could the target lose a limb, suffer from a debilitating accident, break bones, or go through other horrific events?

* **The target will sustain the effects of this spell forever.**
  Forever is an extremely dangerous word. This is not a
  justifiable petition unless harm was caused to debilitate
  you, the spellcaster, for the remainder of your own life.

* **The target will move away.** The term *away* here could
  possibly be interpreted by Spirit to mean just a few
  blocks, a mile, a kilometer, or even just a few houses
  from yours. In the workplace, it could mean a transfer
  to another department in the same building. This won't
  solve your problem.

Instead, word your petitions more specifically to create a
clear, concise request or command. The prior examples can
be readily changed to the following to evade future problems:

* **The target will suffer in the same manner that he
  caused others to suffer.**

* **The couple will break up.**

* **The target will endure the same misery that he caused
  to others.**

* **The target will endure the same pain that he caused to
  others.**

* **The target will sustain the effects of this spell for as
  long as deserved.**

* **The target will move away from (your city or state).** I
  live in Detroit, so my petition would be: "The target will
  move out of Michigan" or "The target will move to Ohio."

* **If it harms none.** Another safe approach is to verbally
  stipulate that there will be no harm to anyone besides
  the target.

Sometimes, Spirit will take matters into its own hands
and deliver a greater punishment than what you had anticipated. If your petition was executed properly and this happens, it usually means you were unaware of the magnitude

of hurt and pain caused to others and not just to you alone. In most cases, the facts will be revealed to you in the future.

In the next chapter, we'll look at petitions in greater detail. But, for now, just contemplate the consequences of open-ended statements.

Step 6. Know What Times Are Best to Cast Negative Spells

It is traditional in numerous spiritual practices to perform spells during specific moon phases and days of the week. As a Hoodoo practitioner, I adhere to these practices because of the assistance provided by the energies emitted during these specific times. Additionally, by waiting for the ideal timing, it provides the practitioner a window for optimal preparation.

However, always remember, when an emergency occurs, you do not need to be concerned about spell timing. If your physical well-being or life is in danger, notify the proper authorities and begin spellwork immediately. Otherwise, perform your spells under the following guidelines.

Moon Phases

The waning moon phase, which starts two to three days after the full moon and lasts until the day before the new moon, is said to hold banishing energies that eliminate or remove unwanted people or situations, as well as delivering destructive energies.

However, many spellcasters will begin negative spellwork on the first night of the full moon. This is because the full moon holds a lot of power and has always been associated with aggression, insanity, violence, and other strange behaviors in both humans and animals. Therefore, it is believed that negative spellwork is assisted by this moon phase.

Days of the Week

The best days to begin and enforce negative spellwork are Tuesdays and Saturdays.

* **Tuesday** is ruled by the planet Mars and represents conquering and power over enemies, war, and violence.
* **Saturday** is ruled by the planet Saturn and represents banishing and endings.

Many practitioners will also work with times when the hands of the clock are moving downward as a ritually symbolic gesture of decreasing or ridding oneself of someone or something. Others will also work with hourly planetary alignments, which can be found on astrological websites or books.

When to Avoid Spellwork

* **Mercury in Retrograde:** Mercury is the planet that fosters communication. Three or four times a year for a three-week period it will appear to be moving in the opposite direction as viewed from Earth. During retrograde, there are interferences in communication resulting in confusion. We will find that others either don't understand the verbal or spiritual messages being conveyed or there are misunderstandings. Spellwork ought to be avoided during this time of confusion.
* **Solar or lunar eclipses:** While many spiritual practitioners believe that these events are times of gathering great power, most Hoodoo practitioners believe that during an eclipse, the energies of both the sun and the moon are blocked. In ancient times, witches didn't cast spells during an eclipse because they believed it represented discord.

The Best Day of the Year to Perform Any Spellwork

Once, or sometimes twice, a year, the full moon will fall on the astrological house of your personal moon sign. It is said that on this day, if Mercury is not in retrograde and there are no lunar or solar eclipses, your chances of successful manifestation are optimal. This is your day, and you can perform any spell you wish. The sky is the limit!

Another Great Day to Perform Spellwork

As both Halloween and All Saints' Day approach, the veil between this mundane world and the spiritual world thins, which facilitates our ability to communicate with entities. The full moon closest to October 31 is another great day to cast a spell and will result in heightened chances of successful spell manifestation.

Step 7. Know Your Battlefield Soldiers: The Spiritual Court

Often, when an injustice has been served to someone, it leaves that person feeling desperation, despair, and/or isolation. While in this state of mind, many clients erroneously profess that "God isn't watching over me," "God doesn't care about me," or "nobody hears me when I pray so, why bother?"

These typical proclamations are most often simply feelings of isolation, induced by either stress or depression after having been accosted. This mental state normally last for about two weeks then will gradually subside.

The fact is that you are not alone, and you have never been alone. All humans are gifted with Guardian Angels, the spiritual entities assigned to each individual at birth and tasked to remain with us, as well as protect us, throughout our lives. This is referenced in Psalm 91:11 of the Holy Bible (KJV):

For he shall give his angels charge over thee, to keep thee in all thy ways.

We also have Spirit Guides readily available to us. Unlike our Guardian Angels, they do not provide protection. Instead, they act as our mentors when guidance is required.

We have the ability to call on our Guardian Angels and Spirit Guides, as well as other entities whenever we desire or need assistance. This is our personal spiritual court, which also consists of:

* The god or gods of your religion or spiritual practice.

* The goddess or goddesses of your religion or spiritual practice.

* The archangels in heaven.

* The saints.

* The deities of your religion or spiritual practice.

* Your ancestors whom you know to have loved you.

Getting acquainted with one, a few, or several the members of your spiritual court prior to initiating spellwork is important, because you will then have an established rapport. Later, it will be easier to call on them when assistance is needed, which will be discussed in the following chapter.

But for now, call upon the ones who make you feel most comfortable by their proper names or titles. Set up a little private area in your home to offer white candles and fresh water to them. Introduce yourself and speak aloud with humility and respect, as if you were speaking to your own parents. Continue familiarizing yourself with them until you sense their satisfaction.

The Five Don'ts of Summoning Entities

1. Never summon aloud using the following dangerous words: "I call on anybody who will help me." This is a huge mistake because it offers an invitation to any entity, especially negative ones, who may respond under the guise of being helpful. Remember, when you are performing negative spellwork, they will already be trying to lurk around your workspace, which is why we will first establish cleansing and protection rituals.

2. Never call on entities that are foreign to you. There are ancient entities who require sacrifices and will take their due—which may be your own blood or worse—if it is not willingly offered.

3. Never make open promises such as "I will do anything if my petition is granted" or "I will do anything to be vindicated." This is an unlimited open-ended sacrifice.

4. Never recite prayers or words in languages you do not know, despite what you may have been told. Additionally, do not take someone else's interpretation of the meaning on blind faith. Research the words yourself, and if you feel uncomfortable, don't say them. Personally, I believe that deities understand all languages so it's not necessary recite languages that are foreign to you.

5. Do not call in evil entities for assistance. People are often under the misconception that doing so will facilitate negative magic. It will instead cause problems for those who do not know how to control them, and most will not leave when dismissed. An old witch once told me, "When evil's asked to come and play, it's hard to make them go away."

Take your time to review all of these steps. Unless it is an emergency, there's no reason to immediately rush into spellwork. Fast and sloppy spellwork can manifest consequences that you do not want. Time, on the other hand, is your friend because it offers you a period to prepare for revenge in a meticulous fashion, leaving no stone unturned.

The Bare Essentials

Now that you have developed a sensible strategy, it's time to select a working space and acquire objects or items connected to or associated with the wrongdoer—who from here on in will be referred to as the *target*. It will be imperative to have a clean working area, as well as a cleansed body and soul. Most importantly, it is crucial to protect yourself, your home, and those who live with you from any potential physical or spiritual hazards.

This chapter will provide you with the bare essentials needed to perform negative spellwork both effectively and safely. You will also learn how to call on your spiritual court for assistance in a manner that could compel them to take pity on you and help unconditionally. Once you have mastered these techniques, you will be ready to cast your spells without fear or reservation.

The Hoodoo Altar

Many spiritual practitioners have stunning, if not breathtaking, elaborate altars. There is also a spectrum of excellent books published on this very topic. But in the practice of Hoodoo, a sophisticated workspace is not necessary.

The old Hoodoo practitioners were either enslaved people who kept their magical practices hidden or, later in the twentieth century, impoverished people. They had no resources or means to erect ornamental altars and made do with what they had. Yet, their spells nevertheless worked.

Hoodoo altars are simply a space—usually a raised area but that's not always required—for a religious or spiritual ritual. They can be fancy and ornate or just plain and unassuming: the choice is yours. All that really matters is the intent and treating the area with respect and reverence.

For indoor altars, you could use:

* A table
* A workbench
* A bureau
* A desk
* A sink
* A bathtub
* A shower (remove the shower curtains first)

Please do not use areas, such as closets, that are close to anything that could catch fire or get contaminated with negative spiritual energies. Do not place an altar in the immediate area where your family, friends, or pets frequent. Pets could easily dismantle it, and if you carelessly expose your spellwork to others, it will result in curiosity, intrigue, and, ultimately, gossip. It's worth mentioning again: always keep your spellwork hidden!

Additionally, the adverse energy particles from negative spells can attach themselves to any living creature that happens to be around if they are not protected. There have been several times I have found dead insects in and around my working space during or after performing cursing spells. Unfortunately, they were in the line of fire and vulnerable. Therefore, the very first essential rule is to ensure that, for their safety, you have no pets, children, or adults in or around your immediate working space.

Do not work negative magic concurrently with positive magic—such as love, prosperity, or success spells or anything of an affirmative nature—on the same altar. Most spiritual practitioners have distinctly separate areas. They use one room or one side of a room for negative magical spells and another room or another side of the room for positive magical spells. When the weather is tolerable, I prefer working my negative magical spells outdoors. Outdoor altars may include:

* A patio table
* A porch or deck
* A backyard
* A barbecue pit
* The ground
* A wooded area
* A secluded area in a park
* A graveyard

For cursing rituals, you can place either a black or white cloth—as white is a neutral color—over the surface. Although optional, ritual items could be placed in a pattern that works with the cardinal directions:

* **Incense** would be placed on the east side of the altar to represent air.
* **Candles** would be placed on the south side to represent fire.
* **Liquids** would be placed on the west side to represent water.
* **Herbs and minerals** would be placed on the north side to represent earth.

There are numerous spells that do not require an altar. Some examples include incantations using petition papers, freezer spells, or torturing a doll. There are also direct contact spells that may include laying a trick—often called contagion magic by anthropologists or contact work by Hoodoo practitioners. Laying a trick is simply to deploy a magical item where the target will directly or indirectly interact with it. They may do so by stepping on it, touching it, passing near it, or consuming a nonpoisonous substance. There are numerous modes of deployment, but never send a child or a pet to transport tricks as they could be negatively affected by the magic.

Obtain Your Target's Personal Concerns

Personal concerns are items that have been directly connected to your target whether biologically or by long contact, most often containing their DNA (deoxyribonucleic acid) molecules that are each individual's personal blueprint. Some folks refer to these as *taglocks*. When casting spells on someone, their personal concerns are the most potent materials to acquire because these contain an essence of that person. Having a personal concern allows the spellcaster to assert their domination over the target. The two most easily accessible items to obtain are hair and skin cells:

* **Hair:** There are about 100,000 hair follicles on each human being's scalp. The average person sheds about 100 strands of hair a day. But, because of daily heat styling and frequent hair coloring, women tend to lose more hair than men. If a person is suffering from impending alopecia, malnutrition, or various other physiological ailments, they will lose even more hair in a day. Of course, hair on other parts of the body is shed frequently as well.

* **Skin cells:** Human beings shed approximately 30,000 to 40,000 skin cells an hour. When removing your slacks, for instance, have you ever seen powdery flecks on the fabric and wondered what it is? What appears to be powder is actually millions of skin cells. What about that ring around the bathtub? No, it's not all dirt: it's mostly skin cells! Why does excessive dust accumulate

so rapidly in your home when you keep a clean house? Again, dust is mostly comprised of human skin cells.

When an object is handled or touched for a short period of time, the transfer of skin cells—called touch DNA—does not always occur. According to *Forensic Magazine*, studies showed that twelve out of thirty subjects transferred little to no DNA onto a sterile tube after handling it for ten seconds. So unless a fingerprint is left behind, if the target simply touches something, that object will not carry a personal concern.

Of course, if you acquire a secretion belonging to the target, then it's obviously a conquest! And that brings us to other personal concerns besides hair and skin, which include:

* Blood
* Dandruff
* Earwax
* Feces
* Fingernails
* Fingerprints
* Footprints
* Mucus
* Saliva

* Scabs
* Semen
* Sweat
* Tears
* Teeth
* Toenails
* Vaginal secretions
* Urine

Please remember not to combine your target's DNA with your own. For example, if you are a woman planning to perform negative spellwork on a man, do not collect his sperm from your own body after sex because it will also contain *your* essence. If you are a man, your penis will also carry your own seminal secretions. Except for toilet spells or urinating to assert domination, do not combine your DNA with negative ingredients because you will also be negatively affected by the spell.

Adjuncts to Personal Concerns

These are traditional items that have been in contact with, or represent, your target. Although they have a weaker connection, these have sufficed in thousands of spells. Utilize them along with the personal concerns or, if you can't get access to the target for personal concerns, by all means use the adjuncts:

* **Your target's full birth name and birth date:** If you know the birth name of your target's mother, it adds more power to the spell. So, for instance, if your target's name is Jane Doe and her mother's maiden name is Mary Earnoselips, you would state: "Jane Doe, born February 31, daughter of Mary Earnoselips."

* **A photograph of your target:** Ensure that eyes are showing because the eyes are the windows to one's soul.

* **Your target's signature:** Photocopies of the signature are extremely weak adjuncts, and I never use them.

* **Your target's handwriting:** Again, photocopies are weak links.

Where to Acquire Personal Concerns

My clients are always surprising me with their ingenious tactics to acquire personal concerns. The following are just a few ideas for obtaining them, but be creative in your pursuits:

* **Ashtrays:** Peel the paper off the cigarette butts as they have an abundance of skin cells from the lips as well as saliva.

* **Beds:** Sheets and pillowcases are loaded with hair and skin cells. They may also contain genitourinary secretions. If you cannot take the materials, use a lint remover or tape to pull up the hair and skin cells.

* **Combs and hairbrushes:** Look for hair. Brushes will also contain skin cells.

* **Garbage cans:** These are treasure chests of personal concerns. They may contain used Kleenex, tampons, sanitary napkins, condoms, Q-tips, and other gems. I consider them to be gold mines!

* **Hamper:** Dirty clothing is also loaded with skin cells and hair. Dirty underpants may contain feces or genitourinary secretions. Please note that washed clothing will no longer contain personal concerns.

* **Razors:** Wipe them down with a clean white tissue or rag as they are also loaded with hair and skin cells.

* **Sinks and sink traps:** These areas typically contain mucus along with skin cells, hair, and sometimes urine.

I do not recommend toothbrushes or washcloths to acquire personal concerns as the detergents in both toothpaste and soap will destroy the skin cells. Additionally, the water used for rinsing will dissolve or eliminate them.

Never use all of your acquired personal concerns for one spell. Additionally, do not send all that you've acquired to a for-hire spellcaster. You may need them for subsequent spells.

Handling Personal Concerns

After obtaining your target's secretions, they may be refrigerated for a couple of days. After that period of time, they ought to be air-dried on a white tissue or a small piece of white cotton cloth. Otherwise, secretions such as urine will turn rancid and emit a horrific odor.

But if you've acquired personal concerns from a love interest, do not freeze them for future use. Placing a personal concern in the freezer will freeze that person out of your life.

When making an effigy of your target, such as a clay doll, never bake the doll because it changes the composition of the DNA and will no longer contain an essence of your target. Think of it in these terms: What happens after baking, boiling, or frying raw meats or produce? The consistency changes because the DNA has been altered. To avoid any problems, use air-drying clay.

Petition Papers

A petition paper contains either a request, command, prayer, or glyph. My preference is to use torn pieces of brown paper bag, while avoiding the manufacturer's designs, lettering, cuts, or folds, and inscribing the petition with a pencil or a fine point marker. Avoid using ink pens as they tend to skid on the paper bag losing letters, or even words.

In the Hoodoo tradition for negative spellwork, the target's name is written either nine or thirteen times, once on each line. Turn the paper ninety degrees to the left and write a brief command, usually one to five words, directly over the name, to assert domination over the target. This is again written nine or thirteen times, one command on each line. I prefer writing the person's name in pencil and the command with a fine point black marker, but the choice is yours.

Next anoint the petition paper with either a condition oil that correlates with your spell's intent, such as Banishing Oil to make someone or something go away or almond oil mixed with the appropriate herb that correlates to your condition, such as asafoetida (*Ferula assa-foetida*), an herb commonly used in banishing spells.

Anoint your petition paper with the oil in five areas, commonly called the "5-Spot" pattern: upper left hand corner, upper right hand corner, lower right hand corner, lower left hand corner, and finally, the middle of the paper.

Fold the paper once away from you, then turn the paper to the left and again fold it away from you. If this is a large piece of paper, you may repeat the process once more but avoid too many folds as it make the petition paper too bulky to sit appropriately under or in the assigned location in the spell instructions.

In other African Traditional Religions, such as Santería, a petition is constructed differently. You would write out the target's birth name, followed by the birth date and the desired command. For instance, if John Doe were a threat at your workplace, your petition would look something like this:

John Doe

Born July 20, 1808

Will be fired from the Ford Motor Company

Another method is to write the open petition paper as a letter to the entity who is being asked for help. They will sometimes enclose the petition within four crosses if it is a Catholic saint being petitioned. I have done this several times throughout my life and have achieved successful results. Since my patron saint is the Virgen de la Caridad, I will include her in the next example:

+

My Dear Virgen Caridad del Cobre

John Doe, born July 20, 1808

Is threatening my job security.

+ *Please have John Doe fired from Ford Motor Company* +

Because he will cause my job loss.

I love you with all of my heart and soul

Your Daughter,

Miss Aida

+

These petitions are kept open and placed under a statue or framed picture of your preferred entity or under a candle dedicated to that entity. Anointing the paper in a 5-Spot pattern is optional, then the paper is placed in the assigned location.

For the sake of convenience, I usually prepare several petition papers on the same target in one sitting. Then I store them in a sealed plastic bag. This is because I usually perform more than one spell on a target to achieve a cumulative effect that will penetrate through their aura.

Spiritual Cleansings

Now that an altar has been established and you have acquired your target's personal concerns and/or adjuncts and have prepared your petition papers, you must ensure that you and your space are spiritually pure. Interferences from lingering energies may cause your spells to be obstructed, damaged, or to go awry. The procedures to take care of this are neither time-consuming nor complicated.

Cleanse Your Workspace

Your workspace must first be cleansed of any negative energies presently residing there. These energies may interfere with your spellwork and bring about undesired results. Additionally, you may have shed your own hair or skin cells in the space, and these will get contaminated with the negativity from your spellwork if they aren't removed before you begin.

Negative energies latch on to living and nonliving hosts and like to hide in piles of clutter. So ensure that your space is clear of clutter, and try to keep it as free from other unnecessary items to avoid contamination.

Prior to and following spellwork, clean as many surfaces as possible with Chinese Wash, which removes negativity. You may purchase it from a reputable spiritual store or make your own. Follow this up by pouring Florida Water into a spray bottle or filling the bottle with one teaspoon of sea salt mixed with two cups of water and spraying it around the area. Avoid spraying wood with Florida Water; it is alcohol-based and can ruin your furniture.

Trust me, you will notice a huge difference in your environment with these magical cleansers!

Miss Aida's Chinese Wash Recipe

One 32-ounce bottle of Murphy's Oil Soap

One ½ ounce bottle of quality Van Van Oil

2 ounces of liquid pure castile soap (to dilute the Murphy's Oil Soap)

One frankincense incense tear (to enhance the power of the formula)

1 tablespoon of lemongrass herb

13 new broomstraws (aids in spiritual cleansings)

A little bit of your saliva

Remove about three ounces of Murphy's Oil Soap from the bottle to make room, then add the Van Van Oil and castile soap to the bottle. Agitate the bottle to disperse the liquids. Add the frankincense tear, followed by the lemongrass, then the broomstraws. Replace the cap and gently shake the bottle.

Once it appears that the lemongrass has been dispersed, remove the cap. Place your mouth close to the lip of the bottle and recite a blessing prayer or Psalm 23 aloud. Then respectfully release a little of your saliva into the bottle to activate or charge the ingredients. Your Chinese Wash is now ready.

Use about one-quarter cup of Chinese Wash per bucket of water. A new mop is preferable for the floor, but a clean mop will suffice. You will also need clean rags to wipe down other surfaces.

PSALM 23 (KJV)

1 The Lord is my shepherd; I shall not want.

2 He maketh me to lie down in green pastures: he leadeth me beside the still waters.

3 He restoreth my soul: he leadeth me in the paths of righteousness for his name's sake.

4 Yea, though I walk through the valley of the shadow of death, I will fear no evil: for thou art with me; thy rod and thy staff they comfort me.

5 Thou preparest a table before me in the presence of mine enemies: thou anointest my head with oil; my cup runneth over.

6 Surely goodness and mercy shall follow me all the days of my life: and I will dwell in the house of the Lord forever.

Spiritually Cleanse and Protect Your Aura

Negative forces can affect us in many ways ranging from mild—such as feeling drained or having a run of bad luck—to severe—spiritual attacks. These incursions suppress our aura, the spiritual shield that protects us.

If you are performing justified negative spellwork, then your aura has already been attacked because someone had emotionally or physically assaulted you. A suppressed aura, in turn, leaves one vulnerable to further damage because negative energies attract the same.

Retaliatory spellwork involves working with unfavorable elements, so you must begin with a clean, healthy, and vibrant protective shield. Then protect your aura to deter these elements from affecting you.

Spiritual Cleansing Baths

Spiritual cleansing baths are intended to clear the aura of negative energies adhering to it and are not meant to remove the daily physical dirt that our bodies naturally accumulate. Therefore, if needed, take a regular bath or shower to remove physical dirt or grime at least a few hours prior to any spiritual bath.

Precautions

Please keep in mind that if you have open sores or wounds on your skin, including rashes, avoid any spiritual cleansing baths until you have first consulted with a physician. Also ensure that you have no allergies to any of the bath ingredients before you engage in a bath with these ingredients.

Bath 1: Holy Water Bath

Fill a bathtub with warm water.

Add four ounces of Holy Water to the bathtub water and agitate the water to disperse it.

Bath 2: Ammonia Bath

Fill a bathtub with warm water.

Add only one tablespoon of ammonia to the bathtub water and agitate the water to disperse it.

Remember the adage "more is better" does *not* apply to ammonia. Do *not* increase the amount of ammonia as it is a skin irritant.

Bath 3: Sea Salt Bath

Fill a bathtub with warm water.

Add one-quarter cup of sea salt to the bathtub water and agitate the water to evenly disperse the salt.

Bathing Instructions

Remove clothing and enter the bathtub nude. Immerse yourself, head included, a total of thirteen times while reciting aloud Psalm 37, which speaks of harmful people who have hurt you. Prior to closing the recitation with the word *Amen*, state your plea to remove all negative energies from your aura. If you are wearing hair extensions or weaves, only immerse yourself up to your neck. Attempt to remain in the bathtub for thirteen minutes.

Once you are ready to leave the bathtub, do not rinse yourself off. Instead, walk out of the bathtub and lightly blot yourself dry, preferably with a white towel. Put on your clothes. Remove the bathtub stopper and as the water drains, state aloud that all negative energies are to leave immediately. Anoint the back of your neck and head with Protection Oil, Blessing Oil, or Holy Oil for protection. If oils are not available, spray Holy Water on these areas.

PSALM 37 (KJV)

1 Fret not thyself because of evildoers, neither be thou envious against the workers of iniquity.

2 For they shall soon be cut down like the grass, and wither as the green herb.

3 Trust in the Lord, and do good; so shalt thou dwell in the land, and verily thou shalt be fed.

4 Delight thyself also in the Lord: and he shall give thee the desires of thine heart.

5 Commit thy way unto the Lord; trust also in him; and he shall bring it to pass.

6 And he shall bring forth thy righteousness as the light, and thy judgment as the noonday.

7 Rest in the Lord, and wait patiently for him: fret not thyself because of him who prospereth in his way, because of the man who bringeth wicked devices to pass.

8 Cease from anger, and forsake wrath: fret not thyself in any wise to do evil.

9 For evildoers shall be cut off: but those that wait upon the Lord, they shall inherit the earth.

10 For yet a little while, and the wicked shall not be: yea, thou shalt diligently consider his place, and it shall not be.

11 But the meek shall inherit the earth; and shall delight themselves in the abundance of peace.

12 The wicked plotteth against the just, and gnasheth upon him with his teeth.

13 The Lord shall laugh at him: for he seeth that his day is coming.

14 The wicked have drawn out the sword, and have bent their bow, to cast down the poor and needy, and to slay such as be of upright conversation.

15 Their sword shall enter into their own heart, and their bows shall be broken.

16 A little that a righteous man hath is better than the riches of many wicked.

17 For the arms of the wicked shall be broken: but the Lord upholdeth the righteous.

18 The Lord knoweth the days of the upright: and their inheritance shall be for ever.

19 They shall not be ashamed in the evil time: and in the days of famine they shall be satisfied.

20 But the wicked shall perish, and the enemies of the Lord shall be as the fat of lambs: they shall consume; into smoke shall they consume away.

21 The wicked borroweth, and payeth not again: but the righteous sheweth mercy, and giveth.

22 For such as be blessed of him shall inherit the earth; and they that be cursed of him shall be cut off.

23 The steps of a good man are ordered by the Lord: and he delighteth in his way.

24 Though he fall, he shall not be utterly cast down: for the Lord upholdeth him with his hand.

25 I have been young, and now am old; yet have I not seen the righteous forsaken, nor his seed begging bread.

26 He is ever merciful, and lendeth; and his seed is blessed.

27 Depart from evil and do good; and dwell for evermore.

28 For the Lord loveth judgment, and forsaketh not his saints; they are preserved for ever: but the seed of the wicked shall be cut off.

29 The righteous shall inherit the land, and dwell therein for ever.

30 The mouth of the righteous speaketh wisdom, and his tongue talketh of judgment.

31 The law of his God is in his heart; none of his steps shall slide.

32 The wicked watcheth the righteous, and seeketh to slay him.

33 The Lord will not leave him in his hand, nor condemn him when he is judged.

34 Wait on the Lord, and keep his way, and he shall exalt thee to inherit the land: when the wicked are cut off, thou shalt see it.

35 I have seen the wicked in great power, and spreading himself like a green bay tree.

36 Yet he passed away, and, lo, he was not: yea, I sought him, but he could not be found.

37 Mark the perfect man, and behold the upright: for the end of that man is peace.

38 But the transgressors shall be destroyed together: the end of the wicked shall be cut off.

39 But the salvation of the righteous is of the Lord: he is their strength in the time of trouble.

40 And the Lord shall help them, and deliver them: he shall deliver them from the wicked, and save them, because they trust in him.

Hide Your Work

Many practitioners will create a circle of sea salt or sulfur around their workspace to both hide and protect their work from being revealed to psychics or unwanted entities. In Hoodoo practices, it is common to place bay leaves on the four corners of the room and/or on the altar to keep work hidden. I emphasize wearing bay leaves in your shoes because you minimize your chances of being revealed by the living or the non-living even if you're not using an altar and just laying tricks.

Protect Yourself and the Space Around You

When performing negative spells, remember that negativity attracts the same. It is possible to attract adverse energies and unwanted entities who will try to harm anyone—including you. Therefore, not only is it essential to hide your work but also to place barrier shields at doorways, windows, and on yourself, as if you were erecting a massive spiritual steel wall and donning a bulletproof vest.

Making straight lines with a protective agent across door thresholds, windowsills, and near other entrances, such as near fireplaces, acts as both a barrier and deterrent for unwanted energies. Some of the most commonly used protection agents employed as barriers include the following:

* **Black salt** is used in negative spells but also works to drive away evil.

* **Holy Oil** has a connection with God.

* **Protection Oil** keeps away harmful energies.

* **Rue Oil** is used for protection and eliminating harmful energies.

* **Sea salt** will do anything that you will it to and also drives away negativity.

* **Sulfur** drives away any unwanted negativity and kills jinxes.

Refrain from Using Alcohol and Drugs

Alcohol, as well as benzodiazepines (such as valium), barbiturates, and opiates, are central nervous system (CNS) depressants that slow down brain functioning.

Another widely used CNS depressant is marijuana, which is also classified as a mild psychedelic drug. The New Health Advisor shares in an article that research has proven marijuana will exacerbate conditions such as anxiety, depression, and other emotional alterations. If you are reading this book, you have most likely been victimized by a wrongdoer, so my educated guess is that you are already experiencing extreme anxiety.

Creating more of the same is not a prudent thing to do.

Therefore, don't perform spellwork while under the influence of alcohol or drugs. It interferes with your concentration and also weakens your energy output—essential to manifest your spells, as well as to protect yourself from predatory entities.

Also beware of pseudo-spiritual practitioners who consistently indulge. It speaks volumes on the quality of their spellwork.

I am not suggesting you must completely cut alcohol or other legal recreational drugs out of your life. Just avoid them while performing spellwork or calling on spiritual assistance.

Strengthen Your Protective Shield with Creative Visualization

Now that your working space is protected, start your self-defense tactics by utilizing this effective technique that has been employed for centuries. You may see this called an energy shield, psychic protection shield, or simply a light shield.

Simply go to a quiet place, take a few deep breaths to calm yourself down, and relax for a couple of minutes. Then close your eyes and visualize a bright white light surrounding your feet, visualize the light moving upward until your entire body is engulfed with it.

Although the light is sufficient, you may also wish to visualize protective symbols floating within the light. My preference is to picture tiny crucifixes, and sometimes I will also visualize Jesus Christ smiling at me.

If you employ this technique as directed, once you open your eyes you will actually feel the light surrounding you. Then it's time to don a protection amulet.

The Protective Power of Amulets

Amulets—arising from the Latin root *amuletum,* meaning "an object that protects a person from trouble"—have been utilized for centuries due to their power in protecting the bearer by emitting specific defensive vibrations. Amulets are employed by almost every culture around the world and exist in many varieties. Most amulets are worn by the bearer and may include gems, coins, pendants, rings, written words, and plant parts such as roots. The following are the most typical types of amulets.

* **Spiritual deities:** The image of a sacred deity is said to be infused with their powers.

* **Religious or spiritual symbolism:** These could be images such as a crucifix or any other sacrament that contains a representation of protection.

* **Pentagram of Solomon:** One will protect the wearer from curses and evil spirits.

* **Mirror charms:** Worn or pinned to your garment, these reflect negative energies back to the sender.

* **Protection crystals:** Crystals such as amber, amethyst, black tourmaline, jade, jet, obsidian, and tigereye can also be set in necklaces, bracelets, earrings, rings, and other jewelry.

* **Lockets:** Written petitions or protection herbs such as rue, rosemary, or agrimony as well as other objects

empowered for protection may be kept inside the locket and worn as a pendant.

* **Master Root:** This will protect both men and women. As an amulet, carry a whole root piece.

All amulets ought to be cleansed before wearing as we do not know who has handled them before us. Cleansing them by lightly spraying with either Florida Water, a little sea salt mixed with water, Holy Water, or whiskey will effectively rid them of negative energies. Follow up by anointing the amulet with a little protection oil while reciting Psalm 91— one of the most powerful prayers of protection in both the Hebrew Bible and the Christian Old Testament. Or pray a protection prayer from your own spiritual or religious beliefs. If a protection oil is not readily available, the protection prayer will be sufficient.

PSALM 91 (KJV)

1 He that dwelleth in the secret place of the most High shall abide under the shadow of the Almighty.

2 I will say of the LORD, He is my refuge and my fortress: my God; in him will I trust.

3 Surely he shall deliver thee from the snare of the fowler, and from the noisome pestilence.

4 He shall cover thee with his feathers, and under his wings shalt thou trust: his truth shall be thy shield and buckler.

5 Thou shalt not be afraid for the terror by night; nor for the arrow that flieth by day;

6 Nor for the pestilence that walketh in darkness; nor for the destruction that wasteth at noonday.

7 A thousand shall fall at thy side, and ten thousand at thy right hand; but it shall not come nigh thee.

8 Only with thine eyes shalt thou behold and see the reward of the wicked.

*9 Because thou hast made the L*ORD*, which is my refuge, even the most High, thy habitation;*

10 There shall no evil befall thee, neither shall any plague come nigh thy dwelling.

11 For he shall give his angels charge over thee, to keep thee in all thy ways.

12 They shall bear thee up in their hands, lest thou dash thy foot against a stone.

13 Thou shalt tread upon the lion and adder: the young lion and the dragon shalt thou trample under feet.

14 Because he hath set his love upon me, therefore will I deliver him: I will set him on high, because he hath known my name.

15 He shall call upon me, and I will answer him: I will be with him in trouble; I will deliver him and honor him.

16 With long life will I satisfy him and shew him my salvation.

Remember to pray aloud, and prior to ending any prayer with an *Amen*, ask to be protected from harmful energies, entities, and people. Be respectful, be humble, and show gratitude. Most importantly, have faith that your prayer is being heard.

For more magical protection techniques, as well as uncrossing spells, see my book *Hoodoo Cleansing and Protection Magic: Banish Negative Energies and Ward Off Unpleasant People.*

Summoning Your Spiritual Court

As discussed in chapter 1, each individual has a vast array of entities to call upon for help with spiritual quests, ranging from revered deities to personal entourages. Now that you have selected the spirits you will call for assistance, the following are a few suggestions on how to work with these entities.

Pray Aloud Once, But Ask Three Times

No matter whom you choose to assist you, the prayers and petitions you have for them must be verbalized aloud. My mother was a witch born in the early 1920s in Cuba. Lacking a formal education, it was easy for her to explain the "how-to" but difficult to explain the "whys." She used to tell me that if I don't pray or state my petitions aloud, nobody would hear me and my desires would not be manifested. She also demanded that I pray once but make my request three times. She could not tell me the rationales behind these beliefs, but later in life, I learned that sound is energy, frequency, and vibration. Sound is, in fact, power that emits into the universe.

In college, we were taught that Nikola Tesla (July 1856–January 1943) was one of the greatest minds and inventors of all time and known as "the genius who lit the world." But what they didn't teach us is that he was also a spiritual man. Two of his many famous quotes, cited on Goalcast.com, include: "If you want to find the secrets of the universe, think in terms of energy, frequency and vibration," and "If you only knew the magnificence of the 3, 6 and 9, then you would have the key to the universe." He did everything in sets of three, including making calculations in the environment to ensure that the results were conceivable by that number. And of course six and nine are divisible by three.

Never in my wildest dreams could I have ever imagined that my mother, a witch, and Nikola Tesla, one of the greatest scientists and inventors of all time, had so many core beliefs in common! I wonder what they would have said about this? Could these types of happenstances reveal that the alleged superstitions of yesteryear just might be the scientific realities of the future? Only time will tell!

Whatever the case, thousands of spiritual practitioners from past to present honor the power of three, and there's obviously credibility in its effectiveness. As a side note, in the Hoodoo tradition, practitioners work with odd numbers, beginning with the number three, and later in this chapter, you'll learn more about this technique.

Explain Yourself

Whether you are performing a positive or negative spell, most entities will not blindly grant your request without knowing a reason for your appeal. Therefore, you need to explain it out loud for them. Explanations serve a threefold purpose:

* They justify your work to the entities.
* They engender pity for you from the entity, and you may possibly acquire more forceful assistance.
* They remind you of the hurt and anger of the situation, and this anger will be passed on into your spells as more energy emitted back into the universe to affect your target.

Calling Your Guardian Angels, Spirit Guides, or the Deceased

Calling in your Spirit Guides, Guardian Angels, and/or ancestors isn't complicated. They are already nearby. So just call on them aloud three times, explain your dilemma, what you plan to do (called the verbal petition), and ask them for assistance. Again assuming as an example that John Doe is trying to take my job from me, here is what I might say:

I call upon my Spirit Guides! I call upon my Spirit Guides! I call upon my Spirit Guides! Please hear me. I have been an honest and loyal employee of the Ford Motor Company for ten years. John Doe, born July 20, 1808, is a treacherous swindler and has been lying about me to my superiors in order to get me fired so he can assume my position. I am casting this spell to instead get him fired and ask for your assistance. John Doe will be fired from Ford Motor Company! John Doe will be fired from Ford Motor Company! John Doe will be fired from Ford Motor Company!

Note two important details:

1. The Spirit Guides were called three times to ensure I have gained their attention.
2. My verbal petition of the outcome I want was stated three times.

Calling on Revered Deities

In Christian and other practices, people appeal to deities through prayer—which is another formula of words. There are different patterns for each deity, but nonetheless, all prayer serves as a formal invocation addressed to a specific revered spirit in order to personally petition them as a solemn request for help, to express gratitude, or just to communicate.

How to Pray

Throughout the years, I have witnessed many people pray incorrectly by rapidly reciting memorized words in a monotone fashion while lacking any feeling, meaning, or thought. They follow this by stating their petition just as flaccidly. Then they later wonder why their prayers weren't answered.

Deities must be approached with respect, humbleness, and humility, and prayers must be recited slowly and with passion. Envision what you are reciting. If you are calling on a saint, envision their presence. Feel that entity in front and around you and be honored and humbled by that presence.

Effective praying means knowing that you have been heard. In other words, you must have faith that the communication took place. When we have doubts or pray without conviction, usually nothing will happen. We know how this goes as human beings: When someone asks us for help in a robotic manner, we tend to ignore them because we sense a lack of sincerity in their pleas. But if they are humble, respectful, and ask with conviction, we will most likely assist them. The same is true when petitioning deities.

The content of the prayers that you are reciting also ought to be strongly visualized as well. In Verse 2 of Psalm 23, for example, it says: "He maketh me to lie down in green pastures: he leadeth me beside the still waters. . . ." When I say this, I always envision myself lying in beautiful green pastures while God stands next to me. Then he motions for me to follow him and leads me to the most beautiful blue waters I had ever seen.

After the prayer and before closing with *Amen*, I plead passionately—as a child begs a parent—for assistance. Many rootworkers maintain that if we beg God and/or the saints, they will respond with the love and pity that a parent would have for their own flesh-and-blood child. Approaching them in this manner compels them to help us.

St. Michael

Michael is an archangel in the religions of Judaism, Christianity, and Islam. Christians believe him to be a spiritual warrior in the battle of good versus evil and a champion of justice. He is frequently summoned by numerous Hoodoo practitioners when an injustice has been served by an evil person or when defense is needed from attacks by unseen evil forces.

Prayer to St. Michael

This is the most common invocation to St. Michael. Remember to call his name three times before reciting the prayer and to tell him who you are, explain the situation, and state your petition three times before closing the prayer with *Amen.*

> *Saint Michael the Archangel, defend us in battle. Be our safeguard against the wiles and wickedness of the devil. Restrain him, O God, we humbly pray, and do thou, O Prince of the heavenly Host, by the power of God, cast into Hell Satan and all the evil spirits, who prowl upon the world seeking the ruin and destruction of souls.* **(now, state your case and plead your petition).** *Amen.*

Other Revered Deities

These are many other deities who will assist you in battle as well as protect you. For a complete list of these entities, I highly suggest the *Encyclopedia of Mystics, Saints & Sages: A Guide to Asking for Protection, Wealth, Happiness, and Everything Else!* by Judika Illes. It is a treasure chest of information. More prayers will be provided in later chapters.

Express Gratitude

Once your petition has been granted, be sure to express your gratitude by lighting another candle, serving a fresh glass of water, and providing offerings pleasing to the entity you petitioned. Some saints prefer coffee or liquor; others prefer flowers or sweets.

Knowing Your Candles Intimately

I n spiritual practices, candles serve several purposes. For example, they are lit to commence ceremonies or rituals, employed to honor or petition entities, used to represent deities, and set aflame to energize spells. Their energy can also nourish entities.

As soon as we light a candle or oil lamp for ritual purposes, the flame pierces the veil between this mundane world and the spiritual realm, facilitating the communication of our spoken words and through the tools and ingredients of our spellwork. So when a flame is lit, we are simultaneously opening a doorway to the other realm as well as emitting power to energize both the spell and the spirits being petitioned.

Entities communicate feedback through the candle flame, the wax symbology of the candle itself, and if a container is used, such as a glass vigil candleholder, the behavior of the residue within the container.

This chapter will attempt to teach you not only how to work with candles effectively but help you to understand why certain techniques are used. Additionally, we'll look at candle communication in an effort to help you identify, recognize, and interpret this language.

Start with a Virgin Candle

A virgin candle is one that has never been previously burned or used as an effigy for a different purpose. Always begin a new spell with a brand-new unbroken candle. A used candle will have deeply absorbed the energies from its previous functions as well as particles from the environment to which it had been exposed. For similar reasons, do not use candles you've received as gifts in spellwork. You just don't know where these have been and the type of energies they may have picked up. Perhaps someone may have placed a spell on that candle or even made it from leftover wax from previous spells.

Types of Candles for Negative Spellwork

A *vigil candle* is a candle encased in a glass holder. These are sold as three-day, five-day, seven-day, and nine-day candles. Usually, the nine-day vigil candles correlate with the intention of performing a novena or nine-day petition.

A *taper candle* is a long cylindrical candle available in a variety of sizes. For instance, *chime candles* are the simple four-inch taper candles most commonly sold. Six-inch and nine-inch candles are also readily available. I vehemently oppose the use of the thinner, shorter *birthday candles* in spellwork because they can't be inscribed or dressed, and their combustible time is limited to just a few minutes. This does not give the practitioner enough of a window to pierce the veil and communicate with entities effectively, nor do they provide enough power to energize both the spell and the spirits.

My preference for helper lights to surround the main spell in the center of the altar is chime candles. Some Hoodoo practitioners assign or correlate the numbers nine or thirteen with negative spellwork. So for instance, when performing a negative altar spell, I could have twelve chime candles encircling the main candle, for a total of thirteen.

Figural candles, often called *image candles,* are those shaped or carved into a likeness or representation of what they wish to manipulate. Many practitioners who work unusual or extremely strong spells prefer them because their symbolism is easy to see and thus helps the practitioners focus on what they wish to influence.

Figural candles are also available as *effigies,* which represent a specific person—or people if the candle has two images. Those that are shaped as a man or woman are frequently used in lieu of cloth, clay, or other dolls. When a candle will be employed as an effigy, as with dolls it ought to be baptized to bring an essence of the target's spirit into it. Once it is baptized, it need not be lit if you intend to treat it as if it were a doll.

For negative spellwork, the most common candle color is black, representing banishing or menacing intents. If black candles are not available, white is neutral and can serve as a substitute for any color. Although there are an array of various and ingenious candle images on the market, those often found in negative spellwork include:

* 7 Knob Wishing Candles
* Back-to-Back Divorce Candles
* Bride and Groom Candles
* Female candles
* Heart candles
* Lovers candles
* Male candles
* Penis candles
* Skull candles
* Vagina candles

Always remember, as with dolls, an effigy candle with an image of one person can represent no more than one person. If the effigy candle represents two people, it may only be assigned to two specific people and cannot be later reused to represent other people.

Trimming the Wick

Almost all candles are sold with extra-long wicks. Trim them down to expose only a quarter of an inch to prevent high flames, smoke, and wick knotting. In my experience, once a wick begins knotting, it will continue to do so even with continuous trimming.

Cleansing Your Candles

Energy attaches to an object if a person has handled it for prolonged periods of time, and candle wax is particularly suited to absorb such energy. Would a candle used for love work provide a successful outcome if it had been handled by someone emitting negative energies? Or could a candle for negative spellwork bring a successful outcome if it has only been handled by someone who is in love? Of course not!

Additionally, only God knows where any hands may have been prior to handling a candle, and they may have passed on dormant bacteria. Although factory-produced and wrapped objects may not have been directly handled by anybody, it's better to be safe than sorry by cleansing your candles prior to initiating spellwork.

I spray my candles with either Florida Water or sea salt water prior to working with them. Then wipe off the moisture with either a clean white towels or paper towels, or set the candles directly on the towels and allow them to air-dry.

Inscribing Your Candles

Inscribing a candle is simply writing a command on the candle, and if you are using a figural candle, you will also inscribe the target's name and birth date. The rationale behind inscribing candles is that as the candle wax is being consumed, the energy of the command will be released into the spirit world. Hoodoo practitioners use pencils, pins, needles, knife points, or coffin nails to inscribe candles. I prefer a pencil because it is easy to handle and minimizes the chances of slippage when writing.

The inscription on your taper candle will only contain the command. For positive spellwork, the candle is inscribed starting from the bottom and continuing toward the top to represent attracting something to you such as love, success, money, and all things favorable. Conversely, inscribing a candle starting from the top and continuing toward the bottom represents removal, banishing, or menacing requests.

Since the numbers nine and thirteen are implemented in negative spellwork, the command ought to be inscribed on the taper candles the same amount of times. However, it is virtually impossible to inscribe a command nine or thirteen times on chime candles—there's not enough surface area—so three times will suffice for them.

The command to inscribe on the candle, as well as on your petition paper, will correlate to the intention of your spell. If, for example, your desire is to break up a toxic relationship, your command of "break up" would be inscribed on the candle nine to thirteen times, from the top to the bottom, in spiral fashion, without lifting your pencil between words. It would look something like this:

breakupbreakupbreakupbreakupbreakupbreakup
breakupbreakupbreakup

If you are working with a figural candle, inscribe the target's name, followed by their birth date, three times, once on each line. Then turn it to the left and cross over the names with the command three times one line beneath the next for a total of three lines. The result ought to look like a square that contains words. For this case we are only doing things three times because—unless the candle is gigantic—there won't be enough surface area for nine or thirteen commands. However, you can also continue to write the command independently all over the surface of the candle to enhance your intentions.

Blessing or Baptizing Your Candle

Taper candles or figural candles that are not used as effigies can be charged or blessed to infuse more of your energy into them. To charge a candle, visualize volts of electricity running down your arms and into your hands. Once these volts are in your hands, clutch the candle and visualize it absorbing the electricity. If you have performed this procedure correctly, you will feel just a tad weak from the transfer.

Blessing a candle is to use your own god- or goddess-given power to do so. Hold the candle in one hand, and make the sign of the cross with your index and middle fingers of your other hand while stating aloud: *"By the power invested in me, I bless you in the name of the Father, the Son, and the Holy Spirit. Amen."* If your spiritual beliefs differ from Christianity, bless the candle according to your own faith.

A figural candle in the form of an effigy such as men, women, or skull candles ought to be named and baptized, just as you would name and baptize a doll. The acts of baptism and naming summon an essence of the target's spirit into the object, thus making it a part of them.

Hoodoo practitioners use water, whiskey, Florida Water, Holy Oil, or Holy Water for baptismal rituals. I prefer Holy Water from a Catholic church, an Eastern Orthodox church, or Lourdes, France, because its authenticity is assured. Holy Oil, such as from a church, is equally effective. The first rain in the month of May is also considered to be Holy Water. I anoint my right index and middle fingers with the Holy

Water, hold the effigy in my left hand, and make the sign of the cross directly on the crown of the effigy's head with the fingers of my right hand while saying aloud: "I baptize you in the name of the Father, the Son, and the Holy Spirit. Amen."

If an effigy only represents one person, implement this naming ritual. Assuming that my target's name is John Doe, I would hold the effigy in both of my hands and envision his face. Then I would continue holding the effigy and raise it up facing the sky or ceiling, while envisioning electrical volts arising from my shoulders and moving through my arms, into my hands, and on into the effigy while screaming, "And I name you: 'John Doe, John Doe, John Doe . . .'" (screaming his name for a total of nine times).

If the effigy represents two people such as a bride and groom, lovers, or a married couple, the naming ritual differs. Rather than holding it up facing the sky and screaming the target's name into the tool, instead place the face of the first image in front of your lips and state: "I name you (target's name)," then repeat the steps with the other image's face.

Finally, breathe life into the effigy by saying: "I now give you the breath of life." Then place your mouth directly over the effigy's mouth, and blow air into it. It's an exhausting ritual, but you will have transmitted a lot of energy into your effigy, making it a very effective tool.

Dressing Your Candle

Dressing a candle is anointing it with an oil, and then if desired, rolling or dusting it in crushed herbs or incense. Candles are dressed to give them, and your spell, extra power.

Anointing Your Candle

The most popular types of oils for anointing candles for spellwork are either olive oil, which is frequently mentioned in the Holy Bible, or an oil that matches the correlating condition for your spellwork. For instance, if the intent of the spell is to send someone away, the condition is to banish or hot foot that person. So an oil called Banishing or Hot Foot Oil works with the correlating condition of your intent. Condition candles, sachet powders, soaps, perfumes, and bath crystals are also available from spiritual shops.

In the Hoodoo tradition, such oils are also known as conjure oils, hoodoo oils, dressing oils, or ritual oils. No matter what they are named, if you opt to purchase a condition oil in lieu of using olive oil, ensure that you are getting quality products that contain herbs and/or an essential oil that correlates to the condition.

Anointing a candle typically follows the same directions as inscribing it: to attract favorable desires you would anoint the candle starting from the base and continuing up to the wick, but for removal, banishing, or menacing requests, you would go in the opposite direction starting from the wick and continuing down to the base of the candle.

This is just a symbolic gesture. If you make an error in the anointing process, just use your fingers and correct the direction. And if the candle has already been consumed, don't be overly distressed—I seriously doubt that Spirit would deny the request just because the candle wasn't anointed per symbolic protocol.

Due to their large surface areas, figural candles typically necessitate a higher volume of oil. Quality condition oils are expensive, and we often waste oil when we overestimate the amount needed or our fingers absorb a large quantity of it. I have found aspirating the condition oil into a 1 cc syringe, discharging it over the candle surface, then ritually anointing it to be cost-effective because the oil is being applied directly onto the candle and not your much larger skin surface areas. Additionally, a 1 cc syringe is perfect for the application of oil directly into a candle, as you will later see in the vigil and skull candle preparations.

If you decide to roll or dust your candle with incense or crushed herbs, you must do so immediately after the anointing procedure to ensure attachment to the candle. By waiting too long, the oil will either dry or absorb into the candle within a few minutes, and that will hinder the adhesion process.

Rolling or Dusting Your Candles

It is believed in the Hoodoo tradition—as well as many other practices—that plants, roots, and minerals possess magical properties. These elements have spirits that can be awakened and called upon for assistance in spellwork, even after death or dormancy.

A condition incense may contain herbs or essential oils, but one of its main purposes is to communicate intentions into the universe through the element of air. It is believed that spirits are attracted to its smoke as well as its odor and respond accordingly.

If you choose to dress your candle with herbs, you must first finely crush them. Then awaken their spirits by placing them close to your mouth and reciting Psalm 23 aloud while remembering to visualize what you are praying. Then before ending the prayer with *Amen,* ask God for assistance. As an example, this is what I always say:

> *Father, I am your daughter, Miss Aida. Please awaken these plants and minerals and thank them for having sacrificed their lives for me. Then please give them the power to assist me with my intentions of (specific goal).*

Then I tell God what help is needed from their spirits. Afterward, I thank God and end my petition with *Amen.* If you are of a different faith, pray to the deity that you honor.

If you are using a taper candle, spread the incense or crushed herbs over a paper towel. After anointing your candle with oil, immediately roll it over the herbs or incense.

When using a figural candle, lay the candle on a paper towel and disperse your herbs or incense evenly over the candle with your fingers. The candle is now ready for spellwork.

Transforming a Vigil Candle into a Condition Candle

A plain vigil candle will still serve its purpose if you have prepared your verbal and written petitions correctly. However, if you want to convert a candle into a specific condition candle—called a *fixed vigil candle* by spiritual practitioners—you will have added extra energy and power to its intention.

Take a long thin metal barbecue skewer, shish kebab skewer, or a long thin Phillips screwdriver and bore two holes deep into the wax, a half inch away from the wick, on either side. With an eyedropper or a 1 cc syringe, gently drip your condition oil into the holes, making sure not to use more than half a cc in each hole or, if using an eyedropper, no more than seven drops per hole. The adage "more is better" does not apply in this procedure because too much oil or herbs will interfere with the candle communication feedback mechanism by causing black smoke, black or sooty residue on the glass, or insufficient wax consumption.

Next, crush about one-quarter teaspoon of herbs that correspond to the intention of your work and gently distribute them on the top of the candle. Avoid distributing the herbs near the wick because they will interfere with the language of the candle flame.

Then although optional, lightly sprinkle about one-sixteenth of a teaspoon of black or white superfine glitter on top of the candle and over the herbs. Many practitioners believe that glitter attracts the attention of benevolent entities and keeps them nearby. As an added bonus, glitter, along with the herbs and any remaining wax, can also be utilized for interpretations after the candle has extinguished itself.

If a label is desired, taping it to the side of the container is not a good idea because tape cannot hold up against the temperatures of the heated glass and will ultimately fall off. Instead, I have had great success with 5 by 3½-inch self-adhesive shipping labels. These labels are available in sheets that correspond perfectly to the size of printing paper, thus a perfect fit for the printer.

Select a desired image for your label or just print your target's name, birth date, and your desired command above and below the name. For instance, if I wanted John Doe to go away, I might print a label that says:

Begone

John Doe, Born July 4, 1808

Begone

Position your petition paper inside the candleholder, then place the candle directly over the paper. Or obtain a picture of your target with his/her eyes showing. Write your petition on the back of the target's picture. Then write a one-word command over the target's forehead and place the picture, faceup, in the candleholder with the candle directly on the picture.

Once the Candle Is Lit

Remember that the candle flame pierces the veil between this world and the spirit world thus commencing enhanced communication. So everything said after the candle is lit will be heard by spirits. Avoid any conversations with people or pets when near the flame.

When a spouse, child, or pet is on the other side of a closed door making annoying noises, it is instinctual to shout out commands like "No!" or "Stop it!" But if spirits have already initiated assistance and then hear this, there's a strong probability they'll believe that you are instead speaking to them and will either cease support or even vanish. This is one of the main reasons many spellcasters wait to cast a spell until they are alone while ignoring a ringing telephone or text messages.

How to Extinguish a Candle

The only times I will extinguish a candle is if it needs to be relit for a period of time, such as in a 7-Knob Wishing Candle Spell or a Moving Candle Spell. My preference is to leave a candle lit to maintain a continuous flow of energy into the spirit world.

Still, if I must leave my home and cannot place the lit candle in the bathtub or shower, it needs to be extinguished as a fire safety measure. If a candle must be extinguished, never blow it out. There are fire spirits who assist us in spell-work, and blowing out a flame is a pretentious gesture of disrespect toward these entities. This act may even negate the time you've already spent on the spell if the spirits of fire have been insulted. Instead, respectfully announce that you are extinguishing the flame. Then either pinch it out with your fingers or snuff it out with a glass or ceramic cup, dish, or a candle snuffer.

Interpreting Candle Flame Talk

Pyromancy is the term spiritual practitioners use to describe the interpretation of candle flame communication. However, before you dive into this, first consider the physics of the candle placement, the ingredients on or inside your candle wax, and the quality of the wax because they will have a bearing on the candle burn but may not be indicative of candle communication.

Candles ought to be placed away from any drafts such as open windows, air vents, fans, or fast body motions. Wafting airflow will artificially manipulate the candle flame.

If your candle has been dressed in herbs and/or glitter, you will frequently hear popping sounds—usually a few minutes after the candle is lit. If your candle has been stuffed with herbs or petition papers, popping sounds also occur once the flame makes contact with them. When a flame is consuming an ingredient the popping sounds and dancing flame are just simple physics in action.

Also consider the consequences of purchasing low-cost candles. They are usually made of poor-quality wax, and you might see a weak flame resulting in an incomplete candle burn or an immediate pooling of wax, too fast for wax consumption. Frequently, a vigil glass container will shatter. Remember, you get what you pay for!

The Flame

The flame tells the spellcaster a three-part story through its intensity, the sounds it makes, and the direction it is leaning. You will be able to interpret that story once you understand what each facet represents and put the language together to understand what is being said.

A strong flame is a very good sign your messages are being sent to the spirit world loud and clear. It does not necessarily mean your petition will be manifested, but that you have delivered a clear communication.

A weak flame indicates there are problems. The difficulties could result from an incorrect spell, unclear communication, or obstacles. If the flame self-extinguishes, it most likely means you have missed your target altogether or the request is denied. Some practitioners profess that you may attempt to relight the flame a total of three times, while others claim that once it self-extinguishes, it's time to initiate a different spell.

When a flame rises and dips, it is a sign of resistance from your target. But if it's a jumping flame, Spirit is acknowledging you with energy explosions—and that's what we seek with spellwork.

Sometimes the flame will chatter. When this happens, pay close attention to the tone of the chatter as well as the direction the flame is pointing. This is a clear sign of spirit communication. A soft chatter indicates your target is engaging in intimate conversation with another person. Mild and frequent chattering signals someone of dominance is leading your target, which to me suggests that the person of dominance is the obstacle in the spellwork—i.e., a third wheel. Strong chatter is a good sign in negative spellwork because it indicates that your target is engaged in arguments or rage. So as soon as you hear the chattering, immediately look to see if the flame is high or low and what cardinal direction it is pointing to.

East is the direction that rules communication. If the flame leans toward the east while chattering, you may receive some sort of communication from or about your target.

South is the ruler of fire. If a flame leans in this direction during negative spellwork, intensity and raw power are affecting your target.

West is the ruler of emotions. More often than not, you will see the flame move in this direction when the spellwork involves matters of emotional relationships, such as breakup spells. If, for example, there is loud chatter and the flame leans to the west, the spell is manifesting an argument with the lovers. Conversely, if there is soft chatter, the couple is engaged in tender, intimate conversation.

North is the ruler of the physical and materialism. When the flame leans to the north, it is either a sign that your spell has obstacles that are physical obstructions when the flame is low or, if high, your spellwork will manifest.

Candle Smoke

Capnomancy or *libanomancy* is interpreting the movement of candle smoke. Again, before attempting to interpret this, first consider the physical conditions that you ought not misconstrue as spiritual communication. If the wick is too long and has not been appropriately trimmed, expect a high flame that will subsequently emit smoke. When herbs, glitter, or petition papers are burning or if the wick is knotted, smoke will automatically be produced. If none of these factors are in play, then you can begin capnomancy.

A thin straight plume of smoke indicates a good omen, whereas large plumes of smoke signify obstacles. If the smoke wafts toward a cardinal direction, correlate the behavior of the smoke with the interpretations listed previously.

Interpreting Symbols and Symbolisms

Interpreting candle wax remains is called *ceromancy*. But before you start exploring this type of communication, there is one obstacle that must be conquered to become a proficient interpreter . . .

Resist Pareidolia

Pareidolia is a psychological phenomenon in which the human brain sees recognizable images—most often faces— in random arrangements of shapes. According to the article "Pareidolia: Seeing Faces in Unusual Places," published by *Live Science,* a scientific study in Finland discovered that this most often occurs in people who are religious or believe strongly in the supernatural.

One of the best ways to overcome the tendency to see faces in the wax is to initially glance at the wax remains, recognize the face(s) your brain finds in its patterns, then walk away and do not look at it again for a period of time. I usually wait at least twenty-four hours before returning for the interpretation.

Knowing that my brain is preprogrammed to pick out faces and this is not truly communicated by Spirit, I will look at everything else in and around the misperceived face.

Once my brain has accepted the fact it was merely an illusion, the pareidolia begins to dissipate and relevant symbols will appear.

Interpreting Candle Wax Symbols

The wax remains of both taper candles and figural candles almost always contain symbols for spellcasters to interpret. The symbology of ceromancy is identical to that of teacup readings. You can easily find them online; however, my favorite book on the subject—and the one I have frequently utilized as well as highly recommend—is *Tea Cup Reading: A Quick and Easy Guide to Tasseography* by Sasha Fenton. This book is especially helpful because it contains illustrations of each symbol, so if you can't identify a character, it is easy to spot in this book.

Neophytes sometimes have difficulty finding symbols in the wax remains because they may just see globs. Placing a petition paper or a picture of the target directly under the candle before the spell will greatly assist the spellcaster in the communication process. Not only is it another means to provide information, but this also serves to acquire feedback. If the paper is consumed by the flame, it is a clear indication that the spell was communicated in its entirety to the spirit world. It also frequently denotes a great chance of manifestation because the fire usually consumes all the wax, resulting in a clean burn. When the paper does not burn, it is not a favorable sign, but it can be saved for use in another spell. If the wax adheres to the paper, it's an opportunity to deploy the remains in an attempt to foster manifestation—which we'll discuss in the last chapter.

Taper Candles

When examining taper candles—not including jumbo candles—what you will usually see are centerpieces. There could be a circle with an empty center, indicating that there's a great chance of success because the target is not protected, or a circle is filled with wax like an unbroken circle, indicating resistance. An incomplete circle or centerpiece indicates that the spell has had some effect on the target because there was an opening for the spell to take effect.

Look for symbols in or around the centerpiece because these provide details. For example, if a breakup spell was performed on a couple and the center was filled with wax, I would know there were obstacles. If the centerpiece appeared in the shape of a dog or the shape of a dog was nearby, I'd know that a dog denotes loyalty. Therefore, my interpretation would be that this spell will not manifest because there is great loyalty within the relationship.

Sometimes the wax will accumulate on one side of the candleholder or stand, thus the cardinal direction it traveled toward is another form of communication. Also look to see if a symbol is approaching or leaving the center. For example, a car, boat, or airplane facing away from the center may indicate that the target is leaving, whereas, if it is approaching the center, it might indicate that someone is arriving to help the target.

A jumbo candle, if placed in a holder, almost always leaves a mass of wax. Therefore, if the paper underneath does not burn, it is not an indication of failure but just a result of physics. The wax remains will still contain faint symbols, so do examine them carefully.

Figural Candles

The benefit of figural candles shaped or carved in the form of a symbol is that they assist the practitioner to intensely focus on their desires, but the disadvantage is that they are usually not fully consumed during the candle burn, leaving a puddle of wax in all varieties of irrelevant shapes and forms. The practitioner then has to closely scrutinize each and every possible symbol to determine the pertinent ones to determine messages left behind by Spirit. Also keep in mind, if a taper candle is prepared to be free-flowing—meaning that there is no container to inhibit the wax movement—it will frequently behave in the same manner as a figural candle.

What is usually observed, after such candles have self-extinguished, are wavelike symbols resembling mounds or flower petals. If the candle has been set on a jar, the wax will frequently follow one path leaving streams of wax from the candle to the base of the jar.

In order to overcome this nuisance, focus your attention on the area where the candle was initially placed. Look for symbols in and around that area. Then gradually expand your attention outward and continue to look for relevant symbols.

If the wax had seeped to one side, observe the direction followed, then proceed to interpret by the cardinal point. When a figural candle represents two people, such as lovers or a bride and groom, the seepage could represent tears or the unwillingness of one person to let go of the relationship or situation.

Sometimes, when I am performing justified cursing spells on behalf of a client, the figural candle will change its shape after having been burned. They sometimes look like monsters, or unpleasant gestures have been made with their arms. These symbols do not need interpretation because they simply represent the target's true character.

We'll look at skull candles on their own later because they are prepared differently, and the interpretation of the wax remains also differs from other image candles. In my opinion, they are very effective and my favorite figural candles to work with.

Reading the Symbolic Remains of Vigil Candles

Vigil candles are traditionally allowed to remain lit without interference. When vigil candles are extinguished then later reignited, it interferes with the communication process through what is left behind in the container. You might see rings inside the container, wax pooling, or it will negatively affect the strength of the wick.

If I must leave my home, I remove my shower curtains and place the vigil candles inside the bathtub or shower, far from anything that might be flammable. If this is not an option, you must recite your petitions or prayers each time the candle is reignited.

Once a vigil candle has been consumed, the four things to examine are the integrity of the glass, the clarity of the glass, the amount of remaining wax within the container, and the symbols left behind by the wax itself along with the herbs and/or glitter, if you have chosen to utilize them.

The integrity of the glass: Examine the container for any cracks or breakage. If the intent of your spell is to break up a relationship or inflict justified harm on another, then cracked or broken glass indicates the spell will most likely manifest. However, with the exception of only a few other spells such as a Blockbuster spell, cracked or broken glass denotes an incorrect spell, unclear communication, obstacles, or failure of the spell to manifest.

The clarity of the glass: When wax is consumed evenly and in its entirety and the glass appears transparent, it is called a "clean burn" with a very good chance the spell will manifest. If the glass has a smoky color anywhere on it, there are minor obstacles, depending on the location of the occlusion. Black or sooty marks denote major obstacles. Usually, the location of the obscurities communicates where the problems lie:

* If the entire container is obscured, the spell is surrounded by a multitude of obstacles.

* The top, middle, or end of the glass container gives the spellcaster an idea of timing to match in the beginning,

in the middle, or at the end. For example, if there are obscurities at the top of the candle but the glass becomes clear toward the middle and bottom of the container, it would mean that there will be obstacles in the beginning that will later be conquered.

* Smoky, dark colors or excessive glitter or herbs on the sides of the glass correlate to the cardinal direction interpretations given in the flame section.

The amount of wax remaining within the container: Unburned wax indicates the intensity of the candle spell's effectiveness. For example, if a candle is consumed halfway with a clean burn, it indicates that part of the spell will most likely manifest but not its entirety. Thus, more spellwork is indicated. However, if other obstacles are also present, such as cloudy or sooty glass, the spell will most likely fail to manifest.

Wax, herbs, and glitter symbols: Always examine the glass for symbols left at the bottom of container as well as the sides. Don't just assume that they are obstacles, as they may indicate what may happen from a cardinal direction. I once performed an attraction spell for a client, and the glitter that remained formed the shape of a heart on the north side of the container. It felt as if love would come to her from the north. She later met and married a man who had recently moved from Canada!

Recycle Your Glass Containers

Back in the olden days when I was young, glass vigil candle containers were thick, strong, and sturdy. As time has passed and manufacturing companies have sacrificed quality for the sake of profits, these glass containers lack the superiority of the past. It is my suspicion that as more time passes, the quality of today's containers will again diminish. Therefore, it is prudent to save your glass containers for future use.

Remove any remaining wax, herbs, or glitter with hot, soapy water and a washcloth or paper towel. Then fill the container with a mixture of water and sea salt and allow it to sit for a few days. Afterward, rinse it out thoroughly and store it for later.

Just remember that the composition of these containers is usually silicate glass based on the chemical compound silica dioxide or quartz, which is the primary constituent of sand. Most sand, in turn, is also composed of calcium carbonate and was created by coral and shellfish. Therefore, glass is made from life-forms that contain DNA and have memories which will retain the energies invested into it.

Because of this, only reuse your glass containers *for the same spell purposes.* The target need not be the same person, but the intent of the spell must be equivalent to those performed earlier in that given container.

Now that you are completely adept with the intricacies of spellwork, it's time to move on to recipes and spells . . .

Spells to Send Your Enemies Away

S end-away, banishing, or hot foot spells are those employed to remove, dismiss, drive off, or keep a person or situation away. These spells, in my opinion, are virtually innocuous because the intent involves the least amount of harm to the target while still attempting to thwart future confrontations. They are ideal spells to cast for those who fear karmic or deity retribution for any negative intent toward another because they solely focus on keeping a predator at a distance.

These types of spells are a good first line of spiritual defense against certain types of predators including:

Abusers: These are my preferred spells to remove a person who is physically abusive from their victimized partner. If there is an abuser in a relationship, I emphatically implore spellcasters to resist employing breakup spells as an attempt to rescue the victim from the trauma. Breakup spells often promote negative thoughts resulting in arguments. Such aggressive verbal engagements habitually lead to greater consequences for the victim.

Bullies: Those who seek to take out their anger on others who appear weaker, smaller, vulnerable, or unable to defend themselves.

Envious and jealous individuals: These are the people who wish failure for those who possess a material object, skill, or status they themselves have not been able to or cannot attain.

Gossipers: These folks talk eagerly and casually about other people's private lives in ways that might be unkind, disapproving, or untrue. Gossip can hurt relationships and create a climate of resentment or fear, thus causing stress to victims.

Meddlers: Those who try to change or have an influence on matters that are not their concern or responsibility. They especially do this by criticizing their victims in a damaging or annoying way.

Psychic vampires: Bothersome people who pour out all of their problems on the listener while trading energy levels. Knowingly or unknowingly, they are dumping their problems and negativity upon the listener while replenishing their strength with the energy of the listener. Negative entities will also steal energies.

Trespassers: People who have a sense of entitlement and ignore or dismiss social or physical boundaries.

Undesired, uninvited, or overstaying guests: These people, either expectedly or unexpectedly, arrive at a place, such as someone's home, and remain to the point the host no longer wishes for them to stay. Often they expect the host to lower their living standards by playing housekeeper or concierge to their whims.

Later in this book, we'll examine the severer types of predators and look at spells to contend with their intended or actual immoral actions.

Herbs and Minerals to Send People Away

If you are making powders from the following ingredients listed, the herbs and minerals ought to be finely crushed and blessed before their use in spellwork. Once finely crushed, they can be placed on a charcoal disk and utilized as incense (although if I am using gunpowder or sulfur, I just add a pinch as they are highly explosive). I highly recommend these books for a comprehensive examination of herbs, roots, minerals, and animal curios: *Cunningham's Encyclopedia of Magical Herbs* by Scott Cunningham and *Hoodoo Herb and Root Magic: Materia of African-American Conjure* (which is also loaded with Hoodoo spells), by Catherine Yronwode.

* **Asafoetida** (*Ferula assa-foetida*) banishes people or situations.

* **Barberry** (*Barberus vulgaris*) is used for blocking people. Do not confuse with bayberry.

* **Bay leaf** (*Lauris nobilis*) sends people away.

* **Black pepper** (*Piper nigrum*), mixed with salt, will block intruders.

* **Black snake root** (*Cimicifuga racemosa*) will make people move.

* **Cedar wood** (*Cedrus* spp.) gently moves people away.

* **Epsom salts** (magnesium sulfate heptahydrate) causes people to run away.

* **Gunpowder** (a combination of charcoal, sulfur, and potassium nitrate) aids in the swiftness of numerous spells, especially to drive people away.

* **Red brick dust** (a combination of silica, alumina, iron oxide, magnesia, lime) wards off enemies and negative entities.

* **Red onion** (*Allium cepa*) moves your mate away.

* **Red pepper** (*Capsicum annum*) moves people away.

* **Salt** (sodium chloride), mixed with pepper, moves people away

* **Sulphur powder** (brimstone) serves many purposes, including driving off enemies.

* **Sweet gum** (*Liquidamber orientalis*) will move someone out of your life.

Animal and Insect Curios to Send People Away

* **Ants** make people wander.

* **Dirt dauber's nest** drives enemies away.

* **Dog feces**, used fresh, will drive away foes with the stench. When dried, they can be used with other send-away ingredients to aid in effectiveness.

* **Pigeon feces** are used dried to make people leave in a hurry.

Powders, Oils, and Washes to Send People Away

There are numerous quality condition oils, powders, and washes on the market to send people away, but the most widely used products are Hot Foot and Banishing Powders and Oils, Four Thieves Vinegar, and War Water. You may choose to purchase these products or make your own. Just as master chefs have different approaches to recipes, spiritual workers can have their own variations. These are my condition formulas.

Banishing Powder

Banishing formulas are designed to gently send a person or bad situation away. The manifestations from using these formulas are effective but subtle.

4 teaspoons ground asafoetida

1 teaspoon ground black pepper

1 teaspoon ground salt

Mix well. Then recite a blessing prayer over them, such as Psalm 23. Don't forget to state the intention of the powder.

Banishing Oil

Place one-quarter teaspoon of Banishing Powder into a glass bottle containing two ounces of almond oil. Vitamin E oil acts as a preservative, so also add two drops of this to the almond oil. Then recite a blessing prayer. Add one drop of candle wax dye, if desired, as using colors coordinated to a condition will enhance the power of your mix. Place a cap on the bottle, shake it vigorously, and put in a dark cool area. Shake once a day for two weeks. Your oil is now ready for use.

Emergency Banishing Oil

Although not as fervent as the full formula, this recipe can be a substitute for the full formula listed above for anointing petition papers or candles when time and/or supplies are short. Simply mix virgin olive oil with ground asafoetida and stir until there's a smooth and even consistency.

Hot Foot Powder

Hot foot formulas contain more forceful ingredients than banishing recipes. While some practitioners call it a spicier formula, I say that it puts more "zip" in the "zap"!

5 teaspoons cayenne pepper

1 teaspoon salt

1 teaspoon black pepper

1 teaspoon dirt from a railroad track

⅛ teaspoon gunpowder (can be easily extracted from an unused firecracker.)

Gunpowder brings swiftness to a spell or formula, but do not use more than the one-eighth teaspoon prescribed for this recipe. If you dress candles with this formula, too much gunpowder will cause rapid combustion, flames, and smoke when the flame meets the powder. So please be prudent!

Mix well. Then recite a blessing prayer over them, such as Psalm 23. Don't forget to state the intention of the powder.

Hot Foot Oil

Place one-quarter teaspoon of Hot Foot Powder into a glass bottle containing two ounces of almond oil. Vitamin E oil acts as a preservative, so also add two drops of it to the almond oil. Then recite a blessing prayer. You may also add pieces of dried hot red peppers to the mixture to enhance the desired effect. Add one drop of candle wax dye, if desired. Put the cap on the bottle, shake it vigorously, and store in a dark cool area. Shake once a day for two weeks. Your oil is now ready for use.

The Story of Four Thieves Vinegar

Legend tells that back in the olden days, when people were dying from the black plague (an infectious disease caused by the bacterium *Yersinia pestis*), thieves would rob the bodies of their valuables but ultimately die themselves from bacterial contamination. However, four wise thieves came up with a formula for protection against the plague. This formula was later named in their honor as "Four Thieves Vinegar." Throughout the years, there have been some variations to the original recipe, but it remains effective for magical use because of its protection, banishing, and even antimicrobial properties.

Four Thieves Vinegar

8 ounces red wine vinegar

4 cloves garlic, cut in half lengthwise

½ teaspoon asafoetida

⅛ teaspoon cayenne pepper

⅛ teaspoon salt

Place all the ingredients in the glass bottle containing the vinegar. Recite a blessing prayer over it. Then release just a little bit of your saliva into the bottle to activate the formula. Put the cap back on the bottle and shake it well. Keep the jar covered in the refrigerator, and shake once a day for two weeks. Also shake the bottle prior to each use.

War Water

This water is used to cause conflict between people and move enemies away. Make a big batch of it. The shelf life is virtually everlasting.

16 ounces water collected from either a violent storm or from a stump

Hair from both a black dog and a black cat that do not live together

½ cup Spanish moss

2 tablespoons magnetic sand

½ cup white vinegar

13 rusty nails

Pieces of rusted iron

Broken glass

½ teaspoon asafoetida

Now, if you really want to get down and dirty, you can add just a drop of essence of skunk. But be careful and do this outside because it stinks to high heaven!

Place everything in a glass bottle, and recite a blessing prayer and intention over it. Do not release your saliva into this one! Seal tightly with the cap and shake every day for two weeks.

Thereafter, keep refrigerated.

Although not all spells require these formulas, it is a good idea to at least acquire as many of the aforementioned herbs, minerals, and animal curios as possible for your arsenal of send-away spells and for assistance with your spellwork. As previously discussed, the more spiritual help you can acquire, the greater the chances of successful spell manifestation.

Send-Away Prayers

As we've discussed, prayer is a powerful act of communicating with entities for the sake of worship or seeking their assistance. There are numerous references in the Holy Bible to the power of prayer. For instance, the Gospel of Mark 11:24 (KJV) tells us:

Therefore I say unto you, What things soever ye desire, when ye pray, believe that ye receive them, and ye shall have them.

The 150 psalms in the Holy Bible are all prayers written in the form of poems/hymns that are available to help us in times of need or distress. Hoodoo practitioners frequently employ them just as they had been for thousands of years for aid in prophecy, protection, physiological ailments, divination, and even magical purposes—including curses and sending away the ungodly.

Here are two that are effective in driving enemies away.

PSALM 94 (KJV)

1 O Lord God, to whom vengeance belongeth; O God, to whom vengeance belongeth, shew thyself.

2 Lift up thyself, thou judge of the earth: render a reward to the proud.

3 LORD, how long shall the wicked, how long shall the wicked triumph?

4 How long shall they utter and speak hard things? and all the workers of iniquity boast themselves?

5 They break in pieces thy people, O LORD, and afflict thine heritage.

6 They slay the widow and the stranger, and murder the fatherless.

7 Yet they say, The LORD shall not see, neither shall the God of Jacob regard it.

8 Understand, ye brutish among the people: and ye fools, when will ye be wise?

9 He that planted the ear, shall he not hear? he that formed the eye, shall he not see?

10 He that chastiseth the heathen, shall not he correct? he that teacheth man knowledge, shall not he know?

11 The LORD knoweth the thoughts of man, that they are vanity.

12 Blessed is the man whom thou chastenest, O LORD, and teachest him out of thy law;

13 That thou mayest give him rest from the days of adversity, until the pit be digged for the wicked.

14 For the LORD will not cast off his people, neither will he forsake his inheritance.

15 But judgment shall return unto righteousness: and all the upright in heart shall follow it.

16 Who will rise up for me against the evildoers? or who will stand up for me against the workers of iniquity?

17 Unless the LORD had been my help, my soul had almost dwelt in silence.

18 When I said, My foot slippeth; thy mercy, O LORD, held me up.

19 In the multitude of my thoughts within me thy comforts delight my soul.

20 Shall the throne of iniquity have fellowship with thee, which frameth mischief by a law?

21 They gather themselves together against the soul of the righteous, and condemn the innocent blood.

22 But the LORD is my defence; and my God is the rock of my refuge.

23 And he shall bring upon them their own iniquity, and shall cut them off in their own wickedness; yea, the LORD our God shall cut them off.

Psalm 105 was suggested by author and *palero* Robert Laremy in his book *The Psalm Notebook* "to get rid of someone." My clients and I have recited it frequently with great success. As an added bonus, many practitioners also recite this psalm to eliminate high fevers. Remember to explain everything to God before ending your prayer with *Amen.*

PSALM 105 (KJV)

1 O give thanks unto the LORD; call upon his name: make known his deeds among the people.

2 Sing unto him, sing psalms unto him: talk ye of all his wondrous works.

3 Glory ye in his holy name: let the heart of them rejoice that seek the LORD.

4 Seek the LORD, and his strength: seek his face evermore.

5 Remember his marvellous works that he hath done; his wonders, and the judgments of his mouth;

6 O ye seed of Abraham his servant, ye children of Jacob his chosen.

7 He is the LORD our God: his judgments are in all the earth.

8 He hath remembered his covenant for ever, the word which he commanded to a thousand generations.

9 Which covenant he made with Abraham, and his oath unto Isaac;

10 And confirmed the same unto Jacob for a law, and to Israel for an everlasting covenant:

11 Saying, Unto thee will I give the land of Canaan, the lot of your inheritance:

12 When they were but a few men in number; yea, very few, and strangers in it.

13 When they went from one nation to another, from one kingdom to another people;

14 He suffered no man to do them wrong: yea, he reproved kings for their sakes;

15 Saying, Touch not mine anointed, and do my prophets no harm.

16 Moreover he called for a famine upon the land: he brake the whole staff of bread.

17 He sent a man before them, even Joseph, who was sold for a servant:

18 Whose feet they hurt with fetters: he was laid in iron:

19 Until the time that his word came: the word of the LORD tried him.

20 The king sent and loosed him; even the ruler of the people, and let him go free.

21 He made him lord of his house, and ruler of all his substance:

22 To bind his princes at his pleasure; and teach his senators wisdom.

23 Israel also came into Egypt; and Jacob sojourned in the land of Ham.

24 And he increased his people greatly; and made them stronger than their enemies.

25 He turned their heart to hate his people, to deal subtly with his servants.

26 He sent Moses his servant; and Aaron whom he had chosen.

27 They shewed his signs among them, and wonders in the land of Ham.

28 He sent darkness, and made it dark; and they rebelled not against his word.

29 He turned their waters into blood, and slew their fish.

30 Their land brought forth frogs in abundance, in the chambers of their kings.

31 He spake, and there came divers sorts of flies, and lice in all their coasts.

32 He gave them hail for rain, and flaming fire in their land.

33 He smote their vines also and their fig trees; and brake the trees of their coasts.

34 He spake, and the locusts came, and caterpillars, and that without number,

35 And did eat up all the herbs in their land, and devoured the fruit of their ground.

36 He smote also all the firstborn in their land, the chief of all their strength.

37 He brought them forth also with silver and gold: and there was not one feeble person among their tribes.

38 Egypt was glad when they departed: for the fear of them fell upon them.

39 He spread a cloud for a covering; and fire to give light in the night.

40 The people asked, and he brought quails, and satisfied them with the bread of heaven.

41 He opened the rock, and the waters gushed out; they ran in the dry places like a river.

42 For he remembered his holy promise, and Abraham his servant.

43 And he brought forth his people with joy, and his chosen with gladness:

44 And gave them the lands of the heathen: and they inherited the labour of the people;

45 That they might observe his statutes, and keep his laws. Praise ye the LORD.

Group Attacks

Often, one malevolent person will seek out others to join them in their quest to inflict emotional or physical harm on an unknowing victim. This dynamic had always seemed to be an unexplainable and unjust oddity until I found a passage in the book *What Is a Jew?* by Rabbi Morris Kertzer. A disciple of a wise Chasidic rabbi asked: "Can you tell me, Rabbi, why the wicked are always looking for companions while the righteous are not?" The Rabbi responded: "The answer is simple: The wicked walk in darkness, so are anxious for company. Good people walk in the light of God; they don't mind walking alone."

Groups engage in scapegoating to place blame on one person for the wrongdoings, mistakes, or faults of others in order to conceal their own failings, fears, and weaknesses. They can be ruthless in their actions and behaviors.

In an article written by Dr. Neel Burton for *Psychology Today* entitled "The Psychology of Scapegoating," he says, "The ego defense plays an important role in scapegoating, in which uncomfortable feelings such as anger, frustration, envy, guilt, shame, and insecurity are redirected onto another such as outsiders, immigrants, minorities," who are then persecuted with a sense of self-righteous indignation.

Scapegoating usually occurs in groups where people follow a leader. If you are the victim, do not attempt to cast spells on every single member all at one time because the energy you send out will be scattered. Think of your spell as a gun shooting bullets. If you concentrate and aim directly at one target, you're apt to strike it. But if you attempt to strike several targets with one bullet, you're most likely to miss all of them completely. Instead, identify and concentrate on the ringleader and give that person all that magic artillery you've got.

When the spell has manifested, then work on the next person if the ringleader was not the only source of your problems. However, the instigator usually provides the fuel that feeds the fire. If they're gone, the fire usually subsides.

The following psalm is designed to remove a troublemaker from a group while protecting you from these types of people. Pray this aloud every day for nine consecutive days while spraying Holy Water on the back of your head. Casting spells alongside prayers greatly advances achieving a desired manifestation.

PSALM 1 (KJV)

1 Blessed is the man that walketh not in the counsel of the ungodly, nor standeth in the way of sinners, nor sitteth in the seat of the scornful.

2 But his delight is in the law of the LORD; and in his law doth he meditate day and night.

3 And he shall be like a tree planted by the rivers of water, that bringeth forth his fruit in his season; his leaf also shall not wither; and whatsoever he doeth shall prosper.

4 The ungodly are not so: but are like the chaff which the wind driveth away.

5 Therefore the ungodly shall not stand in the judgment, nor sinners in the congregation of the righteous.

6 For the LORD knoweth the way of the righteous: but the way of the ungodly shall perish.

Saint Alexis/San Alejo

St. Alexis, the Catholic patron saint of beggars, was the only son of a wealthy Roman senator. He learned to be charitable to the poor and eventually walked away from all his worldly goods to voluntarily spend the rest of his life among the poor as a beggar himself. He faced constant persecution and ostracism in this life, but remained steadfast. From what he endured, he has great sympathy for those who are also ostracized and will drive their enemies away.

He is very popular among both the Latin and Latin American communities, and his candles, powders, and oils can be purchased in almost any botanica or Latin American grocery store. Known as San Alejo to Spanish speakers, his feast day is July 17, and his candle color is pink.

This ritual of prayers is accompanied by the burning of a San Alejo vigil candle. Continue the daily prayers until the wax is totally consumed and has extinguished itself. Recite the Saint Alexis Prayer once followed by three renditions each of the Our Father, Hail Mary, and Glory Be.

PRAYER OF SAINT ALEXIS TO DRIVE AWAY ENEMIES, ENVY, AND BETRAYAL

Oh, glorious Saint Alexis, virtuous and blessed Saint,

That inspired by the Lord you walked away from family life,

and you knew to give up everything to live alone and in begging.

Blessed Saint Alexis,

You who have the power to move away

Everything bad that surrounds the servants of the Lord,

I beg you to protect and defend me and give me energy, strength, and courage.

Kind Saint Alexis, you who found favor before Mary,

Today I need your help, please don't leave me abandoned.

In all humility I ask you to take away the enemy and evil from my side.

Get me away from Satan, the liars, the ruin of treacherous people,

of curses, evil eyes, and tongues, of the traitors, the slanderers, and the harmful ones.

Get me away from everyone who wants to see me rendered and sunk.

Keep me from envy of evil and injustice

Keep me from jealousy and resentment, rejection and loneliness

Hide me where they can't find me from those who want to cause my downfall.

Oh, Glorious Saint Alexis, called "The Man of God,"

Bring me closer to Jesus and Mary,

so that with their Divine Goodness, they cover me with all their good

to guide me and set me free of all spiritual and earthly evil,

and help me get the grace that I humbly request of you today.

(STATE YOUR PETITION)

Blessed Saint Alexis, by the grace of the blessed Virgin Mary and by the grace of the Holy Spirit, please have mercy on me. AMEN.

OUR FATHER

Our Father, Who art in heaven

Hallowed be Thy Name;

Thy kingdom come.

Thy will be done on earth as it is in heaven.

Give us this day our daily bread,

And forgive us our trespasses, as we forgive those who trespass against us.

And lead us not into temptation, but deliver us from evil.

For the Kingdom and the Power and The Glory are Yours now and forever. AMEN.

HAIL MARY

Hail Mary, full of grace. The Lord is with thee.

Blessed art thou amongst women,

and blessed is the fruit of thy womb, Jesus.

Holy Mary, Mother of God, pray for us sinners,

now and at the hour of our death. AMEN.

GLORY BE

Glory be to the Father, and to the Son, and to the Holy Spirit

as it was in the beginning, is now, and ever shall be, world without end. AMEN.

The Send-Away Spells

Animals, Insects, or Their Curios

Please note that I neither advocate for the pain, suffering, or torment of any living being nor do I promote unnecessary plant, insect, or animal sacrifices. However, seeking their assistance in spellwork is certainly acceptable.

When working with living organisms, respectfully ask for their help. Trust me, they understand what is being said whether by the tone of your voice, your demeanor, telepathy, or the actual spoken words. Speaking to them has never failed me.

When working with an animal curio, consider its nature as a means to complement a spell. Pigeon excrement, for example, is used because the birds are excellent flyers with quick launches; thus when used in send-away spells, it can cause people to move rapidly. Ants wander by nature, regularly relocating to start new nests or tunnels. Stray animals also wander.

Never use cat excrement as a substitute for dog feces. Dogs often eat cat dung because their manure is sweet and therefore not effective for negative spellwork. Also, do not use the curios of your own pets in spellwork because you don't want the magic to inadvertently affect them.

Ants and Dust

Foot track magic with the aid of ants is a common Hoodoo practice, because ants make use of dirt. Such spells involve dropping dirt from the target's foot track into an ants' nest.

However, if you were lucky enough to acquire dust from your target's home—and you already know that dust contains skin cells—drop that into an ants' nest instead. The ants will immediately begin to utilize it while causing your target to feel restless and the urge to move away.

Ants and an Egg to Make Someone Disappear

A Hyatt informant in Waycross, Georgia, said to carry an egg to a red ant mound. Write on the egg the name of the person you want to leave and tell the egg and ants what you want them to do. Poke a hole in the egg and stick that end into the mound. This spell will take a while because the egg will drip slowly, but once the last of it has been eaten, that person will leave.

Dirt Dauber's Nest

Dirt daubers are gentle wasps also known as organ pipe mud daubers. Their nests resemble tubes made out of mud, and you can find them on vertical or horizontal faces of walls, cliffs, bridges, overhangs and shelter caves, or other structures.

Just take a little bit of this mud structure, being careful not to disturb the entire nest, and dry it out in the sun. Then crumble it to a fine powder.

This powder is utilized in numerous Hoodoo spells of both negative as well as positive intents, depending on the formulas. To send someone away, you can mix this into Hot Foot Powder or with any of the previously mentioned herbs and/or minerals to add extra strength to send-away formulas.

Place your desired mixture into a small bottle along with your target's birth name, birth date, and personal concern, if you have one. Shake the bottle every day, for thirteen days, while demanding that the person leave. When the spell is completed, throw the bottle into a sewer.

Bird Feather

If you find a feather belonging to any bird that takes flight, write the name of your target on it with a fine point marker. Pigeon feathers are preferable, but any kind will suffice. On a windy day, release the feather in a direction opposite the target's residence or place of employment and say: "As this bird takes flight away from here, so shall (target's name)."

Female Stray Dog to Send Away a Female Love Rival

Insert a personal concern from your rival, other than blood,* such as skin cells or body secretions into food that can be given to a female stray dog in heat. Be sure the personal concern is harmless for ingestion first, of course. While she's eating the food, say aloud: "As this bitch wanders from stud to stud, so will (target's name)." Your target will wander from man to man.

Male Stray Dog to Send Away a Male Love Rival

Insert a personal concern from your rival, other than blood,* such skin cells or body secretions—preferably his sperm— into food that can be given to a male stray dog. Be sure the personal concern is harmless for ingestion first, of course. While he's eating the food, say aloud: "As this stud wanders from bitch to bitch, so will (target's name)." Your target will wander from woman to woman.

Feed a Pigeon to Make Them Flee

Mix any type of personal concern from your target that is harmless for ingestion with pigeon feed. Feed the pigeon and ask the bird to take the target away from you. When the pigeon flees, so will your target.

Pidgeon or Stray Dog Excrement

Take a small piece of aluminum foil, shiny side up. Mix cayenne pepper, gunpowder, and a personal concern from the target with the excrement of a pigeon or stray dog. Place this mixture on the aluminum foil and wrap it tightly. Pray Psalm 105 over it for thirteen days then throw it in a sewer.

---

* It is believed in many spiritual practices that giving human blood to an animal will cause the animal to follow the owner of that blood.

Bye-Bye in a Bottle, Container, or Jar

Hoodoo practitioners utilize containers such as gourds, boxes, bowls, bottles, or jars for an array of purposes. They can be shaken, buried, hidden near the target, broken, or just kept.

Containers are also frequently deposited in bodies of running water such as streams, rivers, or sewers—oceans and lakes are not commonly turned to because of the nature of their flow—as a gesture to send someone away. Due to the high levels of water pollution, if you use bodies of running water for spellwork, please be mindful of the container size. Glass containers ought not be larger than a two-ounce bottle. Avoid plastic containers as they are neither traditional nor environmentally safe.

San Alejo Powder Spell

This effective spell was taught to me by my Godmother in Santería years ago. The powder is readily available in most botanicas as San Alejo is very popular in the Latin American community.

On a piece of torn brown paper bag, write the target's name with a pencil nine times, one line below the next. Put the paper in an eight-ounce glass of water. Add half a bottle of San Alejo Powder to the water while saying: "As I put the San Alejo Powder into this glass, keep (target's name) away from me." Then recite the San Alejo Prayer as you stir the contents with a utensil.

Place the glass either outside, somewhere out of the rain, or on the ledge of an open window. When the water is three-quarters evaporated, pour the remaining one-quarter mixture, including the name paper, on a crossroads to which you will not return.

Banish by Evaporation

Place a picture of your target with eyes showing in a clear tall drinking glass. In a separate glass, mix six ounces of water with one teaspoon of banishing powder. Pour this mixture into the glass containing the picture. Keep the glass outside, safe from the rain, or on the ledge of an open window. As the mixture evaporates away, so will your target.

Once all the water has evaporated, throw the picture with any remaining ingredients into a sewer, stream, or river and demand that the target disappear from your life.

Four Thieves Vinegar Jar Spell

Place a picture of the target with eyes showing along with their name and birth date in a four-ounce jar containing the vinegar. Shake the bottle every day for either nine or thirteen days while demanding the target leave town or their workplace. After this time, bury the bottle where your target will step on the ground or hide it in the hollow of a tree where your target will pass.

Hot Foot Bottle Spell

Place your target's name and birth date in a very small glass bottle, then add enough Hot Foot Powder to fill it three-quarters full. Secure cap on tightly. Vigorously shake the bottle every day for either nine or thirteen consecutive days while demanding the target leave. Deploy this bottle into a body of running water.

Habanero Sauce Bottle Spell

Obtain a picture of the target with eyes showing. Inscribe across the forehead the target's name and birth date, along with the command that they permanently leave town. Insert this into a bottle of habanero sauce and cap tightly. Take this bottle far from where the target lives or works and bury it.

Barred by the Broom

Brooms, or besoms, have been associated with the practice of magic all around the world for hundreds of years. Brooms show up with rituals for cleansing, purification, and marriages. They can foretell certain omens and create good or bad luck. They can also ban or evacuate visitors.

Get Rid of Unwanted Company

The most popular and simple Hoodoo spells to rid your home of either unwanted company or guests who have overstayed their welcome include these four options:

To Prompt a Guest to Leave:

1. Turn a broom upside down and lean it by the door, and your company will leave.

2. Sweep the floor immediately in front of your guest, and the guest will leave.

To Prevent a Guest from Returning:

1. Turn a broom upside down and lean it by the door. Let the broom fall immediately following the guest's departure, and the guest will not return.

2. Immediately following the guest's departure, sprinkle salt on the floor, following the trail from where the guest was sitting or standing to the door. Sweep all the salt out the door and onto the street while calling on that guest by name and exclaiming they will never again return.

Cast Out with Candles

Although I do not advocate extinguishing candles in the middle of spellwork, the exceptions to my own rule involve working with either a 7-Knob Wishing Candle or a Moving Candle Spell. Both are intended for extended spellwork.

The 7-Knob Wishing Candles are popular with many practitioners and specifically designed for seven-day petitions. They are also inscribed in a different fashion than the typical banishing formula we've already gone over. The Moving Candle Spells, on the other hand, involve the physical and directional movement of a candle on a daily basis.

7-Knob Move Away Candle Spell

1 black 7-Knob Wishing Candle

Banishing Oil

Hot Foot Oil

Petition paper

Photo of your target with eyes showing

Candle snuffer

These candles have seven knobs. To inscribe them, begin with the top knob and write a command on it in a circular fashion following its contour. Then continue inscribing each subsequent knob. The commands can be different or identical. Try not to lift your pencil inbetween words as they ought to connect to one another.

To move the target away, inscribe the command "move" and the destination. For example, if I wanted my target to move to Ohio, my inscription would look something like this: *movetohio*. Then I would work downward, continuing the inscriptions one on each knob for a total of seven.

Starting with the top knob, anoint it with Banishing Oil. Continue downward, anointing the first three knobs with the same oil to gently nudge the target away. Then to give the target a strong push to leave town, anoint the last four with Hot Foot Oil.

Place the picture of your target, faceup, inside a candleholder followed by your folded petition paper. Set the candle over them.

Light the candle and state your petition and/or prayers. After the first knob has been consumed, snuff out the candle. Burn one knob per day for a total of seven days while repeating your petitions and/or prayers each time the candle is lit.

Move Out of Town Moving Candle Spell

1 white male or female figural candle (depending on your target's gender)

Banishing Oil

A simple map of the town where the target resides and your desired destination

Metal cooking sheet

Hot Foot Oil

Candy (if your target likes sweets)

Cigarettes (if your target smokes)

Money—bills and coins

Hot Foot Powder

Fresh dog feces (optional)

Candle snuffer

Prepare the effigy by cleansing, baptizing, naming, and inscribing it. Anoint it with Banishing Oil. Place the maps on the cookie sheet. Anoint the side where the target presently resides with Hot Foot Oil. Place the candy, money, cigarettes, or anything else that is pleasing to the target on the side where you wish your target to reside.

Place the figural candle over where the target presently resides, light the candle, and state your petition. After half an hour, move it two inches toward the desired direction, and sprinkle Hot Foot Powder followed by a little dog feces, if desired, where the candle was previously. Let the candle continue burning for another half hour then snuff it out.

Repeat this ritual every day until the candle has reached its final destination. Then allow it to completely burn out. Cut the map to separate the clean side from the dirty side.

Throw the dirty side of the map in a sewer. Wrap the candle remains in the clean side of the map and bury it far from where the target presently resides in the cardinal direction of the desired destination.

Contact Magic: Laying Tricks

Hoodoo practitioners refer to contact magic as laying tricks, fixing tricks, throwing down, or laying down. All involve inconspicuously placing, burying, hiding, spraying, or throwing a ritual item into an area where the target will likely interact with it. The target may either have direct contact with the item, such as touching or stepping on it, or indirect contact, such as walking over the item or passing near the item.

You can employ any or all of the aforementioned herbs, minerals, or formulas to lay a trick. The following are just a few popular spells.

Artist's Attack

Mix a large amount of any of your tricking ingredients with paint. With your brush, paint a picture, glaze some pottery, or adorn any other object, and present it to your target as a gift. You may even use a quill pen and draw a design on a greeting card with your "tricked" paint.

Drive Your Car Fast and Far

Mix one tablespoon of Hot Foot Powder with eight ounces of warm water. Once the powder has dissolved, pour the mixture into a spray bottle. Spray this mixture on the tires of the target's automobile while commanding that the car quickly take the person away from your town.

Hot Foot Wax Trick Balls

There are two ways of making trick balls. One is with wax and the other with papier-mâché. The hard-wax balls are not permeable to water and will not disintegrate, making them the preferred choice if your target will most likely pick them up. Papier-mâché, on the other hand, will disintegrate when exposed to rain or another water source, causing the tricking ingredient to disperse and providing a larger area and greater chance for the target to step over the trick.

To make wax balls, melt two black chime candles in a small metal container. As the wax begins to cool, remove the floating wicks, and stir in 1 tablespoon of Hot Foot Powder.

Check the temperature of the wax with your fingers to ensure that it is not too hot. Once cooled enough to form balls, do so while verbalizing your petition. When the balls have completely hardened, throw them into your target's yard where they will likely step on or touch them.

To make papier-mâché balls, slightly moisten the paper and paste mixture and combine it with the Hot Foot Powder. Form it into balls and set aside for a day or two in order for the balls to harden.

No Trespassing!

To prevent those pesky neighbors from trampling all over your property, sprinkle barberry on your property's borders while stating your petition. Once they step on the barberry, it will compel them to avoid future contact with it.

War Water

In many African Traditional Religions as well as folkloric spiritual practices, it is believed that contact with broken glass will inflict bad luck. To make someone move while also causing bad luck, pour some of your war water into a small glass bottle and smash it on the target's pathway.

War Water X

With your war water, make an *X* on the target's pathway so that the person will walk over it and feel compelled to leave.

Farewell with Fire or Air

The element of fire classically represents intense energy, passion, and even fury. So why not gain assistance from this remarkable element to add fervor to your spellwork?

The power of air, on the other hand, is the manifestation of movement and communication. With a masculine influence, the element of air aids in the manifestation of dreams and wishes.

Make a Pest Leave You Alone

Sometimes, visitors will never stop talking. So before they begin to steal my energy and wear me out, I will picture flames bursting out of my entire body. Then I picture the flames approaching the targets. This creative visualization technique has never failed me as people will suddenly cease talking, appear confused, then quickly depart.

Business Card Burning

Perform this spell outside. It works with or without the aid of conditioning formulas, but they are preferred. Take the business card of your target. Anoint it with Banishing Oil and burn it while demanding that this person leave the place of employment listed on the card.

The Witch's Cauldron to Rapidly Move a Target Away

A cast-iron skillet or pot

¼ cup Everclear grain alcohol

Picture of your target, with eyes showing, on photo-quality paper

½ teaspoon gunpowder

½ teaspoon ground Epsom salts

Long matchstick or grill lighter

This spell must be performed outside away from anything flammable. Place the cast-iron skillet or pot on a fireproof surface. Pour the grain alcohol in the skillet. Write the target's name, birth date, and your command across the forehead of the picture and place it in the skillet, allowing it to float on the alcohol. Immediately sprinkle the gunpowder and Epsom salts on the picture. With a long matchstick or grill lighter, set fire to the alcohol. Immediately step back at least four feet from the fire as the gunpowder will begin to shoot sparks. As the picture burns, demand that your target immediately move and specify the distance the person is to travel.

Incense Spell to Move

Perform this spell outside. Write a petition paper with the target's name and your command. Then fold it. Place a lit charcoal disc in an incense censer. Put one-quarter teaspoon of Banishing Powder on the charcoal disc, followed by your petition paper, and top it with another one-quarter teaspoon of Banishing Powder. Once the powder closest to the charcoal disc begins to burn, light the remaining powder with a long match or grill lighter. As they burn and smoke is emitted into the air, stating your petition aloud to the element of air nine to thirteen times.

Helium Balloon

Place a petition paper with the target's name and your command on a small piece of paper and anoint it with Hot Foot Oil. Fold it and place it inside the balloon, then fill it with helium. If the balloon is filled at a store, just tell the worker that the paper is a religious tradition to send a private wish to God. Set the balloon free outside while stating that as the balloon takes flight, so will your target.

Flee with Foot-Track Magic

Foot-track magic has been employed around the world both in modern as well as ancient times. One simply works with or obtains either the complete imprint or some of the dirt left in the foot track of your target, depending on the spell requirements.

In unpaved areas, simply scatter dirt over the path that the target is sure to tread, such as directly in front of the driver's door of their car. Immediately obtain the dirt to ensure that nobody else steps on the spot.

Go as the River Flows

Take dirt from the foot track and put it in a small glass bottle. Before recapping it, talk into the bottle and state that the target will move to where the river stops flowing. Secure the cap and throw the bottle into the river.

Go to a Faraway Land

Have a friend or relative living out of state or country send you local dirt from any ground other than their own property. Mix this dirt with the target's foot track dirt. Deploy this by either throwing the dirt on a railroad track or mailing it to anybody living far from you and ask that person to throw the dirt at a crossroad. You can also sprinkle a little of the dirt inside the target's shoes if you have that access.

Stop Them in Their Tracks

This spell was even practiced in old England. If you find a foot track of your target imprinted in the opposite direction of where they work or reside, pound a railroad spike into it while demanding that the target never turn around and travel back. Do not remove the railroad spike. Walk away without looking back.

Red Ant Nest

Obtain dirt from the target's foot track and take it to a red ant nest. Don't forget to ask the ants their permission before you proceed. Tell them the target's name and birth date, and ask them what you wish to be done. Lightly scatter the dirt in and around the nest, remembering not to harm or disrupt the nest or the ants. If possible, offer them a gift, such as a pinch of sugar, sprinkled outside of the nest.

Dr. Duke's Send Spouse or Lover Away Spell

In the book *Mules and Men,* author and anthropologist Zora Neale Hurston interviewed a famous conjure doctor by the name of Dr. Duke. He took her into the woods several times to teach her how to identify herbs and roots for Conjure, as well as explaining the intricacies of his successful spellwork. One such spell was how he had taught this lady to send away her lazy husband who refused to work thus forcing her to support him as well as his vast spending habits.

Dr. Duke told her to take dirt from her husband's right foot track and parch it in a frying pan. Remove the pan from the fire and, when cooled, place the dirt into a dark bottle. Then mix some dirt from a dauber nest with cayenne pepper and parch those together in a frying pan. When this mixture has cooled, also add it to the bottle, then seal it. Next, she was to place the bottle in one of her husband's dirty socks and tie it up.

Taking the bundle to a river at exactly noon, she was to run to the water, swiftly turn her back, and swing the bundle over her left shoulder. As it fell into the river, she was to recite: "Go, and go quick in the name of the Lord." She was instructed to walk away without ever looking back. The spell must have been successful because Dr. Duke never heard from her again!

Spells to Justifiably Bind Your Enemies

S ometimes, send-away spells are not realistically possible. Examples would include situations such as attempting to move somebody away who lacks the financial or physical means to do so, a bully attending the same classes as your child, or a move that would cause harm to another. If obstacles prevent the realization of physically sending the offender away, the next strategic plan is to bind your target.

Negative binding spells are employed to metaphysically restrict or restrain predators from antagonistic intentions, behaviors, or speech destined to financially, emotionally, or physically hurt an innocent victim. Binding spells can be employed as the second line of spiritual defense against gossipers and are especially helpful to prevent further victimization by predators such as abusers, con artists, scammers, liars, thieves, narcissists, sociopaths, and psychopaths who look for prey in the hopes of stealing something of value.

Identifying the Predators and Their Behaviors

Abusers: Emotional and/or physical abusers wish to take away a victim's freedom, self-worth, and/or self-esteem.

Once a victim is identified, abusers immediately, and often masterfully, begin to manipulate and belittle their sense of control. Gradually, they empower themselves by robbing their targets of their self-esteem, which causes the victims to have self-doubt or fear, thus forcing them to rely on the predator for redemption or recovery—which never happens. Instead, during the entire process, the victims' control and well-being have been compromised emotionally, spiritually, and, sadly, often physically.

Con artists, scammers, and thieves: These predators strive to obtain material possessions and/or sexual gratification. Blackmail—the act of coercion through implied or direct threats—is a common technique implemented by con artists and scammers to ensure a continuous inflow of self-serving gains.

Liars: These are people who represent one set of facts, while knowing that a different set of facts prevail. While many folks tell lies or bend the truth occasionally, their intentions are usually harmless, or they do so to protect property, a person, or people. Pathological or habitual liars, those who chronically tell grandiose stories that exceed the limits of believability, are also usually harmless and do so compulsively and from habit.

However, there are those who lie for self-serving purposes. Sociopaths and psychopaths lie incessantly to get their way and do so with little concern for others. Traitors, the worse kind of liars, are those who betray another's trust or are false to a promise, obligation, or duty. *Inferno,* a book written in the fourteenth century by Dante Alighieri, tells of a journey through the nine concentric circles of hell. Dante says that the lowest ring of hell is reserved for traitors—and rightly so!

Narcissists, sociopaths, and psychopaths: Those who may wish to steal one's social or work status, significant other, or family. These people are usually thrill seekers who lack a conscience and use people to achieve their self-serving goals. They possess ruthless ambition, determined to succeed without caring for others, while lacking morals, wholesome values, integrity, and respect. Sadly, we encounter these cruel predators in various settings. Most of them have psychological disorders of a dissociative nature, and we will briefly examine their traits here.

Narcissistic Personality Disorder

Narcissistic personality disorder crosses the border of healthy confidence into thinking so highly of oneself that no one else matters. These people value themselves more than any other person and place themselves on a pedestal. They can fool others by making people think that they are simply confident people. The Mayo Clinic website states "The diagnostic DSM 5 criteria for narcissistic personality disorder (includes these features but does not need to meet all criteria):

* Having an exaggerated sense of self-importance
* Expecting to be recognized as superior even without achievements that warrant it
* Exaggerating their achievements and talents
* Being preoccupied with fantasies about success, power, brilliance, beauty, or the perfect mate
* Believing that they are superior and can only be understood by or associate with equally special people
* Requiring constant admiration
* Having a sense of entitlement
* Expecting special favors and unquestioning compliance with their expectations
* Taking advantage of others to get what they want

* Having an inability or unwillingness to recognize the needs and feelings of others
* Being envious of others and believing others envy them
* Behaving in an arrogant or haughty manner

What's the Difference Between a Psychopath and a Sociopath?

Both of these designations are classified as antisocial personality disorders with few differences between their traits. Many psychiatrists tend to classify both diagnoses together. It has been suggested that psychopaths are born with the disorder while sociopathic behaviors are learned. Sadly, some scientific research speculates that one out of every twenty-four people are sociopaths.

Sociopathic Personality Disorder

While narcissists are more focused on solely themselves and much more blatant in their behaviors, sociopaths can be a lot more deceptive and somewhat sinister. According to Healthguidance.org: "Sociopaths of course vary in their symptoms and might act differently in different cases. However, their main trait is presenting themselves as having the same empathy, feelings and emotions as others when in fact they lack this emotional capacity. They are thus cold and manipulative and rarely see any problem with their actions." Here are a few of the sociopathic traits according to Healthcare.org. Not all the criteria need to be met:

* Lack of empathy
* Cold, calculating nature
* Shallow emotions
* Narcissism
* Grandiose self-image

* Charming
* High IQ
* Manipulative
* Secretive
* Sexually deviant
* Sensitive to criticism
* Despotic/authoritarian
* Low tolerance for boredom
* Impulsive behavior
* Compulsive lying
* Most often involved in domestic violence cases

By examining the traits of these cunning people, it is easy to understand how they could manipulate others with their charming ways and get ahead with their lies and cheating. Many times, they will even attempt to steal your identity by claiming your work as theirs. They will take what is yours and do whatever is necessary to achieve their goals.

They do not care about any consequences to others. Nor do they care about your physical pain, emotional pain and trauma, or any devastation, shock, distress, or grief that they have imposed. If their acts place you and/or your children in poverty, they just don't care.

Do Not Empower Predators!

Often, victims fear retaliation from their assailants if they defend themselves. However, these fears are frequently unfounded because when in a state of fear, the human imagination can create all kinds of unrealistic scenarios, thus granting the perpetrator both undue credit and power over the victim.

Another common behavior displayed by righteous people is to attempt to justify or rationalize these inappropriate actions, but they do so erroneously by believing that everyone abides by the principles of right and wrong conduct. Always consider that most predators do not follow the same moral codes as the rest of us and will repeat their behaviors if they believe that they can do so without consequences. Remember that undeserved and unfavorable actions will most likely be repeated. Thus, binding spells are justifiably warranted to avoid future malicious acts by the offenders.

Man-Made Tools Commonly Used in Binding Spells

Just as pictures or effigies represent people in spellwork, as well as helping the spellcaster to concentrate and visualize intent and desired outcomes, so can tools. The manner in which we would bind a living being to restrict or constrain their actions will be symbolically reenacted in spellwork through tools that represent these means.

Below are some suggestions for binding tools, but don't be limited to this list. Be creative and use your ingenuity to select anything that you believe to be a useful instrument.

* Bottles
* Boxes or cages
* Chains
* Coffin nails
* Duct tape
* Freezer
* Glue
* Magnets
* Mirrors
* Mousetraps
* Needles
* Nets
* Pins
* Rope
* Rusted nails
* Staples
* Sticky cards or papers used for insect traps
* String or thread (preferably black)
* Tacks
* Wires

Natural Binding Elements

* Burrows that have been abandoned by animals
* Cobwebs
* Rocks, large and heavy
* Spiderwebs that have been abandoned
* Twining vines—poison ivy is the best, but wear gloves and protective clothing to prevent contamination by the ivy.

How to Rust Nails

There are a couple of ways to rust nails. The first is to place uncoated nails in vinegar until they rust. My preferred method is to boil uncoated nails in water, drain them but do not blot them dry, and set them out in the sun. Repeat this process for a few days. On the last day, drain the nails and save the rusted water to include in your War Water recipe.

How to Make Coffin Nails

Authentic coffin nails were commonly used in the past to seal pine boxes containing corpses. Decades ago, many of the old pine boxes were not properly buried in the ground, making it easier to obtain the nails. However, in modern times, coffin nails are difficult to get because caskets now have either hinges that create seals or they simply click shut. Additionally, burials are now more permanent. While most cemeteries are guarded with video cameras at the gates, many also close their gates at dusk to avoid vandalism.

If you are fortunate enough to find an authentic dealer of used coffin nails, they can be extremely expensive. Twenty years ago, I had a friend who frequented old graveyards immediately following rainstorms to obtain nails from caskets that floated to the surface. At that time, she charged a hundred dollars per nail.

As a substitute for authentic coffin nails, two of the most common methods employed are to either bury your rusted nails in a cemetery for nine to thirteen days or store your rusty nails in a bag containing graveyard dirt. If you chose the latter method, ensure that the nails are placed in the graveyard dirt for at least nine to thirteen days.

How to Acquire Graveyard Dirt

Graveyard dirt can be purchased from reputable spiritual stores and dealers for general use. However, be aware that there are many disreputable sellers too. One popular fraud-ulent spiritualist buys bags of cheap potting soil and resells smaller bags in the guise of graveyard dirt, realizing a huge profit from this scam. This example is a very good reason to acquire your own dirt.

But ... What If Someone Sees Me?

Before discussing the protocol for acquiring graveyard dirt, I wish to address the most common question people have asked me: "How do I get the dirt without being caught?" I have two different methods and have implemented them both on hundreds of occasions, while never having been questioned.

My first method is to bring flowers and a little hand shovel. Keep a plastic bag in your pocket or purse. Sit by the grave for a period of time before acquiring the dirt. People will assume you are mourning and plan to offer flowers to your loved one. When you are certain nobody is watching, acquire the dirt and, of course, leave the flowers.

The second method is to bring one of my German Shep-herd dogs with me and a clean poop bag. People will see the bag, empty or full, and just assume that it is for, or filled with, dog feces. Some people have even gone so far as to compliment my integrity for allowing my dog to see his deceased loved one while being conscientious of his discard!

Whatever you choose to do, remember that staff will not be scrutinizing every person who visits a grave. They are mainly concerned with vandalism or theft and focus on those who look or act guilty. So conduct yourself in an inconspicuous manner.

Protect Yourself Prior to Entering a Graveyard

My family had always proclaimed that an entity can easily attach itself to the crown of a person's head or the back of their neck. However, if your overall aura or spiritual protective shield has been weakened though physical or psychological assaults, any area can be vulnerable to spiritual attachments. Therefore, prior to entering any area where entities are known to be present, it is essential to protect yourself. This is easy enough to do by either spraying your body with Holy Water or Rue Water or applying protection oils to the head, neck, or other areas of the body that feel weakened. My Santería family always insisted that I place protection ingredients over the crown of my head, then secure them in place by covering my head with a turban. Oils that safeguard against attachments include the following:

* **Blessing Oil** bestows either holy or divine strength.

* **Eucalyptus Oil** contains strong protection properties and has a potent odor.

* **Holy Oil** has either been prayed over by a religious authority or has been prepared according to ancient texts. It has a connection with God.

* **Protection Oil** will contain the proper herbs and/or essential oils that provide protection—there will be some variation in the names.

* **Rue Oil** calls on the influence of the plant rue, one of the oldest and most widely used herbs for both protection and ridding oneself from negative energies.

Types of Graves to Approach for Graveyard Dirt

Although binding spells are considered negative spellwork, you are nevertheless casting them in order to prevent further harm to yourself or your loved ones. Unlike graveyard dirt for cursing or hexing, which would require dirt from unscrupulous entities, the graves to approach here are for those who possess morality, understand the situation, and are willing to help restrain the target from further harmful activities. Therefore, graveyard dirt can be acquired from:

* A person of integrity
* A person who loved you
* A pious person
* A police officer
* A religious person
* A security guard
* A deceased pet who loved you

The Ritual for Acquiring Graveyard Dirt

Back in the olden days, when video cameras and closed gates were uncommon, Hoodoo practitioners would acquire dirt for positive work from a righteous person before dusk and from an evil person right after midnight. In modern times, this type of timing is not an option, thus attempt to do so as close as possible to the symbolic times.

My Godmother in Santería taught me to acquire the dirt directly from the area that coincides with the deceased person's heart. Numerous old-time Hoodoo practitioners profess the same. She also taught me that the person from whom I acquire the dirt should not have been deceased less than a year or more than four. She explained that if we bother spirits within the first year, we may create a ghost, making them unable to cross over. On the other hand, if they have been deceased for more than four years, they may have crossed over to a different spiritual realm.

Now that you know when and where to get the dirt, there are a few strict but simple rules to remember when acquiring it: show respect and humility, explain the situation and your predicament, ask permission, and give payment. Remember that the entity thinks and feels exactly the same as it did when it was alive. So put yourself in its shoes.

If you lived in a very small house and all you had as a worldly possession was a garden with beautiful flowers, you would naturally be prideful and possessive of them. If a stranger came to your garden and just cut some flowers without your permission, you would be angry because you had been robbed!

But what if the same person came to your house, rang your doorbell, introduced himself, told you why he needed flowers, and respectfully asked you to pay for some of them? More often than not, you would agree to the purchase.

The same principles apply to purchasing graveyard dirt. We just don't "steal" dirt and then expect that dirt to do our bidding. This is the reason that we approach gravesites with respect, introduce ourselves, tell the spirit the story, and ask to purchase a little of their property along with asking for their assistance with the spellwork. Then we wait for feelings of either disagreement, an uneasy feeling, or consent. If the deceased consents, we then collect the dirt, express gratitude, and make a payment.

What Type of Payment?

Always leave a dime buried in the spot where the dirt was taken, as it is the mandatory minimum requirement.

However, you can also leave flowers (which is a lovely gesture), a glass of water, or whatever the spirit liked when it was alive. Do not leave alcohol for a nondrinker or anything that the deceased disliked when alive, as doing so is offensive to the entity and may cause spellwork failure.

Cleanse Yourself after Leaving the Graveyard

Unlike entities, energies act as particles that can attach themselves to almost anything animate or inanimate such as hair or clothing. One never knows what type of negative energies may be dwelling in the graveyard and float right onto you or your possessions.

My Godmother also taught me that if one is not wearing headgear such as a hat, they must first symbolically rid themselves of anything that tried attaching itself to the back of the head. With your open right hand, wipe the back of your head. Then flick your hand downward, several times, ridding the energies toward the ground. This symbolic gesture also gives a clear statement to the entities that you are aware of their intentions and will not tolerate them.

Then cleanse yourself and your inanimate objects as soon as possible. This can be done by spraying Holy Water or Florida Water immediately upon your departure from the graveyard. Others will promptly return home, bathe with spiritual cleansing agents, and wash their clothes.

Herbs and Minerals to Bind or Control Behaviors or Speech

As previously discussed, the herbs and minerals ought to be finely crushed if you will be utilizing them as powders or incense. Otherwise, they may be employed as they are. Either way, they must be blessed before implementing them in spellwork.

There is an array of other marvelous herbs, roots, and minerals that can also restrain or restrict actions and behaviors. Listed below some of the most popular and commonly available ones:

Binding or Restricting Inappropriate Behaviors or Actions

* Knotweed (*Polygonum arenastrum*)

Ceasing Gossip or Slander

* Alum (aluminum sulphate)
* Chia seed (*Salvia hispanica*)
* Cloves (*Caryophyllus aromaticus*)
* Slippery elm (*Ulmus fulva*)

Controlling or Dominating Behaviors or Actions

These are the agents that I prefer to deposit over the tools employed to assert authority.

* Calamus (*Acorus calamus*)
* Licorice root (*Glycyrrhiza glabra*)

The Use of Your Urine in Domination Work

Urine is a personal concern employed for many purposes, including capturing an essence of the target's very being. Our own urine, however, is used for spells of dominance. In nature, animals express dominance by urinating. We frequently see male dogs, for example, raising their legs to urinate higher and over the last male dog's deposit while the females will squat to puddle its urine over it. These acts are all expressions of dominance over the last dog.

These behaviors not only occur with dogs, but with most animals. Years ago, I spent three weeks in the Kalahari Desert examining wild animal pack behaviors. Frequently, a male would wander away to breed with a female from another pack. When it returned to its own clan, the dominant female would urinate on him to mark and identify the animal as her possession and assert her dominance over him. People were most likely instinctively programmed to do the same when humankind lived in primitive societies. Thus, the practice of using one's own urine in Hoodoo spells of domination continues to this day.

When to Avoid the Use of Your Urine in Spellwork

Urine is a personal concern and contains the essence of your very being. Never urinate on anything that contains ingredients that will have an effect on you. For instance, if you are working with stop-gossip, send-away, binding, cursing, hexing, or breakup ingredients and your own urine is in the mix, the spell will also affect you because your essence is directly interacting with them. Stating your intention does not negate the fact that your essence is in the mix with the elements that have been programmed to perform the objective.

You may urinate on a target's personal concern or an adjunct, on the target's property, or on effigies representing the target that cannot absorb the urine or have no other products on the outside of them. Also avoid urinating on cloth dolls filled with ingredients meant to negatively affect the target because the cloth will absorb your urine.

Spoil Intentions with Spoiled Milk

Spoiled milk will spoil anything from plans to relationships. It is used extensively in breakup work, as well as ruining any type of malicious intentions toward you—but only those plans you are aware of.

For instance, I once had annoying neighbors with a sense of entitlement. One day, they planned a huge party on their front lawn. The chairs, however, were on my property, and therefore, that party would have extended to my front yard. I set up "No Trespassing" signs, but they were ignored.

Because I keep spoiled milk in my garage for spell-work, I poured the milk along the property line while repetitiously chanting aloud that the party would spoil. Two hours later, without any weather forecast warnings, a violent rainstorm came through that lasted for hours, forcing the partygoers into their garage and home, rather than on my property.

It's not a bad idea to keep spoiled milk on hand for emergencies. However, spoiling milk contains gases that will produce a horrific odor as well as causing leakage from the bottle, so store the container in a sealed airtight plastic bag. Shake before using and open it outside to avoid the noxious fumes dispersing into your home.

Powders, Oils, and Washes to Bind Actions, Behaviors, and Words

There are numerous quality condition powders, oils, and washes on the market for binding purposes. You may choose to purchase these products or make your own. These are my personal condition formulas.

Stop-Gossip Powder

Alum is available in powder form, and as with any of the stop-gossip herbs and minerals, it can be used alone. I like to grind slippery elm and make a powder with equal parts of both.

Stop-Gossip Oil

2 ounces almond oil

2 drops vitamin E oil (serves as a preservative)

1 drop clove essential oil

¼ teaspoon Stop-Gossip Powder

1 drop candle wax dye, if desired

Chia seeds, optional

Add all ingredients to a glass bottle. Then recite a blessing prayer over the formula. Secure the cap on the bottle, shake vigorously, and set it in a dark cool area. Then shake daily for two weeks. Your oil is now ready for use.

Stop-Gossip Spray

Method 1. The easiest method is to dissolve one tablespoon of powdered alum into eight ounces of hot water. Once it is dissolved, pour the liquid into a clean, unused spray bottle and shake. Also, shake before using.

Method 2. Boil eight ounces of water. Once it boils, remove it from the stove. Immediately add one tablespoon of Stop-Gossip Powder, three whole cloves, and a pinch of chia seeds and steep for five minutes. Strain the herbs and pour the liquid into a spray bottle. Respectfully place the herbs outside on the ground, and thank them for sacrificing their lives for you.

Controlling or Dominating Oil

Method 1. Add two drops of calamus essential oil to a glass bottle containing two ounces of almond oil and two drops of vitamin E oil. Add pieces of licorice root. Add one drop of candle wax dye, if desired. Recite a blessing prayer over the formula. Secure the cap on the bottle, shake vigorously, and place in a dark cool area. Then shake daily for two weeks. Your oil is now ready for use.

Method 2. Add two drops of licorice root essential oil to a glass bottle containing two ounces of almond oil and two drops of vitamin E oil. Add pieces of calamus. Add one drop of candle wax dye, if desired. Recite a blessing prayer over the formula. Secure the cap on the bottle, shake vigorously, and place in a dark cool area. Then shake daily for two weeks. Your oil is now ready for use.

Controlling or Dominating Spray

Boil eight ounces of water. Once it boils, remove it from the stove. Immediately add equal parts of calamus and licorice root and steep for five minutes. Strain the roots and pour the liquid into a spray bottle. Respectfully place the herbs outside on the ground, and thank them for sacrificing their lives for you.

Knotweed for Binding Spray

I like to use knotweed as is, due to its entangling and binding nature. Therefore an oil or powder is not warranted. However, you can make a spray with the herbs by boiling eight ounces of water. Once it boils, remove it from the stove. Immediately add a generous amount of the knotweed and steep for five minutes. Strain the roots and pour the liquid into a spray bottle. Respectfully place the herbs outside on the ground, and thank them for sacrificing their lives for you.

Prayers to Stop Gossip

Remember that prior to closing any prayer with *Amen,* you need to tell God what the problem is and ask him what you wish him to do.

PSALM 12 (KJV)

1 Help, Lord; for the godly man ceaseth; for the faithful fail from among the children of men.

2 They speak vanity every one with his neighbour: with flattering lips and with a double heart do they speak.

3 The Lord shall cut off all flattering lips, and the tongue that speaketh proud things:

4 Who have said, With our tongue will we prevail; our lips are our own: who is lord over us?

5 For the oppression of the poor, for the sighing of the needy, now will I arise, saith the Lord; I will set him in safety from him that puffeth at him.

6 The words of the Lord are pure words: as silver tried in a furnace of earth, purified seven times.

7 Thou shalt keep them, O Lord, thou shalt preserve them from this generation for ever.

8 The wicked walk on every side, when the vilest men are exalted.

PSALM 120 (KJV)

1 In my distress I cried unto the Lord, and he heard me.

2 Deliver my soul, O Lord, from lying lips, and from a deceitful tongue.

3 What shall be given unto thee? or what shall be done unto thee, thou false tongue?

4 Sharp arrows of the mighty, with coals of juniper.

5 Woe is me, that I sojourn in Mesech, that I dwell in the tents of Kedar!

6 My soul hath long dwelt with him that hateth peace.

7 I am for peace: but when I speak, they are for war.

Prayers to Bind Enemies

PSALM 94 (KJV)

1 O Lord God, to whom vengeance belongeth; O God, to whom vengeance belongeth, shew thyself.

2 Lift up thyself, thou judge of the earth: render a reward to the proud.

3 Lord, how long shall the wicked, how long shall the wicked triumph?

4 How long shall they utter and speak hard things? and all the workers of iniquity boast themselves?

5 They break in pieces thy people, O Lord, and afflict thine heritage.

6 They slay the widow and the stranger, and murder the fatherless.

7 Yet they say, The Lord shall not see, neither shall the God of Jacob regard it.

8 *Understand, ye brutish among the people: and ye fools, when will ye be wise?*

9 *He that planted the ear, shall he not hear? he that formed the eye, shall he not see?*

10 *He that chastiseth the heathen, shall not he correct? he that teacheth man knowledge, shall not he know?*

11 *The Lord knoweth the thoughts of man, that they are vanity.*

12 *Blessed is the man whom thou chastenest, O Lord, and teachest him out of thy law;*

13 *That thou mayest give him rest from the days of adversity, until the pit be digged for the wicked.*

14 *For the Lord will not cast off his people, neither will he forsake his inheritance.*

15 *But judgment shall return unto righteousness: and all the upright in heart shall follow it.*

16 *Who will rise up for me against the evildoers? or who will stand up for me against the workers of iniquity?*

17 *Unless the Lord had been my help, my soul had almost dwelt in silence.*

18 *When I said, My foot slippeth; thy mercy, O Lord, held me up.*

19 *In the multitude of my thoughts within me thy comforts delight my soul.*

20 *Shall the throne of iniquity have fellowship with thee, which frameth mischief by a law?*

21 They gather themselves together against the soul of the righteous, and condemn the innocent blood.

22 But the Lord is my defence; and my God is the rock of my refuge.

23 And he shall bring upon them their own iniquity, and shall cut them off in their own wickedness; yea, the Lord our God shall cut them off.

PSALM 140 (KJV)

1 Deliver me, O LORD, from the evil man: preserve me from the violent man;

2 Which imagine mischiefs in their heart; continually are they gathered together for war.

3 They have sharpened their tongues like a serpent; adders' poison is under their lips. Selah.

4 Keep me, O LORD, from the hands of the wicked; preserve me from the violent man; who have purposed to overthrow my goings.

5 The proud have hid a snare for me, and cords; they have spread a net by the wayside; they have set gins for me. Selah.

6 I said unto the LORD, Thou art my God: hear the voice of my supplications, O LORD.

7 O GOD the Lord, the strength of my salvation, thou hast covered my head in the day of battle.

8 Grant not, O LORD, the desires of the wicked: further not his wicked device; lest they exalt themselves. Selah.

9 As for the head of those that compass me about, let the mischief of their own lips cover them.

10 Let burning coals fall upon them: let them be cast into the fire; into deep pits, that they rise not up again.

11 Let not an evil speaker be established in the earth: evil shall hunt the violent man to overthrow him.

12 I know that the LORD will maintain the cause of the afflicted, and the right of the poor.

13 Surely the righteous shall give thanks unto thy name: the upright shall dwell in thy presence.

Binding a Hidden Enemy

There are times when we are unsure of the offending person's identity, especially if it is a con artist, scammer, or thief. This awesome prayer helps to bind those cowards who remain hidden. It is from the book *Helping Yourself with Selected Prayers, Volume 2* by Baba Raul Canizares.

PRAYER

With two I thee see, with three I tie thee down whilst drinking thy blood and breaking thy heart in two. Christ rules, Christ triumphs, Christ defends us from all manner of evil. Hidden enemy, I thee defeat with the strength of St. John. I thee defeat with the sword of St. Michael. I thee torment with the help of the Lonely Soul so that not even a bad intention can thou send to me. Amen. (The Apostle's Creed is to be recited three times after each daily reading of this prayer.)

THE APOSTLE'S CREED

I believe in God, the Father almighty,

creator of heaven and earth.

I believe in Jesus Christ, his only Son, our Lord.

He was conceived by the power of the Holy Spirit

and born of the Virgin Mary.

He suffered under Pontius Pilate,

was crucified, died, and was buried.

He descended to the dead.

On the third day he rose again.

He ascended into heaven,

and is seated at the right hand of the Father.

*He will come again to judge the living and
the dead.*

I believe in the Holy Spirit,

the Holy Catholic Church,

the communion of saints,

the forgiveness of sins,

the resurrection of the body,

and the life everlasting. Amen

The Binding Spells

Binding in Bottles, Containers, or Jars

Coffin Control

Many spiritual stores sell inexpensive, very small hinged curios that look exactly like coffins. Insert a picture, name paper with birth date, and/or personal concerns of the target into the coffin while stating that you bind the person from any more intentions of harming you. If you have graveyard dirt, you may sprinkle some of it on the representation of your target before closing the coffin. Keep this in a sealed plastic bag and shake it every day.

Fish Finishes Gossip

Lay out a picture of you target. Draw the letter X with a black marker over the mouth. Spray the entire picture with alum dissolved in water. Then sprinkle dried alum over the entire picture and roll it up. Place this in a dead fish's mouth. Sew the mouth up with black thread while saying that as the mouth of the fish is sewn shut, so will the mouth of (target's name). Thank the spirit of the fish for sacrificing its life for you, and throw it into a river or stream.

Knockout with Knotweed

Perform this spell outside. Obtain a small container that has a lid and place about a half cup of knotweed inside the container. Take a medium-size rock to pound on a picture of the target. Strike the picture with this rock for a total of nine times while demanding, each and every time, that the person leave you alone. Place the picture over the knotweed, then cover it with another half cup of knotweed. Set the rock over the knotweed to keep everything in place to symbolically pin the target down. Replace the lid and bury this in the woods or someplace far away from you.

Loser Lemon Spell

Slice a fresh lemon lengthwise, but do not slice it all the way through in order to keep the lemon attached on one side. Insert a picture, name paper with birth date, and/or personal concern of the target inside the lemon. Close the lemon with a rubber band while stating that people will sour to the target because they are a loser and forever bound from any further harm to you.

Place the lemon in a sheet of aluminum foil, shiny side facing the lemon, and set it outside. Wear hard-soled shoes and oil the sole of your shoe with controlling or domination oil. Then, step on the lemon every day for three days. After this time, bury it in the woods or in a location far from you.

Sour Intents with Spoiled Milk

This spell must be performed outside because spoiled milk has a horrific odor that will linger in your home for hours, if not days. Take a picture of the target with eyes showing. Write the person's name and birth date across the forehead, and insert it faceup in a jar that has a lid. Set rocks over the picture to prevent the picture from floating. Pour spoiled milk into the jar, but only fill it to half its capacity to avoid the lid popping off from the gases produced by the milk. State that you have bound the target and soured any malicious intentions toward you. Secure the lid and keep the jar outside.

Constraining with Candles

A Tarot Card Vigil Candle Spell

Images of Tarot cards are accessible from the internet. You can easily print any of them onto a printing label for use on your glass-encased vigil candle.

Among many Hoodoo practitioners, the most popular image for binding spells is the Eight of Swords, which depicts a person bound and tied to a fence or cage of swords. If desired, glue a picture of the target's face, with eyes showing, over the face of the image, then inscribe the person's name on the label.

Prepare your petition paper with the person's name and the command to be bound, then anoint it with Controlling/Domination Oil. Fold the paper and set it under the candle. Lightly sprinkle the candle with graveyard dirt. Light the candle and recite your prayers and petitions aloud on a daily basis.

Candle Cage Spell

1 black male or female figural candle

12 black six-inch taper candles

Controlling/Domination Oil

Petition paper

The twelve taper candles are to be inscribed with the command *Binded* written nine to thirteen times on each candle, then anointed with the oil. Also prepare your anointed petition paper. The figural candle will be inscribed with the target's name and birth date but not be anointed with the oil.

Set the twelve taper candles as a circle or square. Then, place the figural candle in the center, with the petition paper beneath it, so as to enclose it within the other candles, representing the target captive within a cage.

Light only the figural candle and recite your prayers and petition aloud. When the wax has been consumed down to five inches, light the twelve candles so that they will be taller than the figural candle, representing their dominance over it, while you repeat the prayers and petition. The taper candles will be the last to self-extinguish.

Captivity Candles

Candles are also employed in spellwork without igniting the wick and serve as a replacement for dolls. Here are a couple of ways to work a male or female figural candle for binding purposes.

In both spells, the candle must be inscribed with the target's name and verbally named. Sprinkle knotweed on the candle and then begin wrapping the candle in duct tape as you repetitiously state your petition aloud. Add more knotweed as you continue to wrap it in duct tape. Once the candle and knotweed are completely wrapped in duct tape, here are two spells to assert your domination over it.

Spell 1. Anoint the soles of your shoes with Controlling/ Domination Oil and stomp on the candle every day while stating that the target is binded (or bound) from doing you harm and is under your control.

Spell 2. Keep it in the bathroom on paper towels. Whenever you have to urinate, place the candle under the stream of your urine while stating that the target is binded and under your domination. Return the candle to the paper towels and replace the paper towels regularly to avoid the rancid odor of stale urine.

Once you see that either spell has taken effect, deploy the candle in a sewer.

Confining Cards

For centuries, spiritual practitioners have employed cards for both divinatory as well as spellcraft purposes. They have done so successfully, for both intentions, because each and every card carries a different energy that can either be interpreted, utilized, or delivered.

My personal preference is the Rider-Waite Tarot deck, originally published in 1910. This deck contains simple images with an abundance of symbolism in the background. I have been using this deck for more than forty-five years with great success in both prophecy and spellwork. For spellcasting, the cards that I most frequently use for binding purposes are:

From the Major Arcana

* XII—The Hanged Man: To represent suspension
* XV—The Devil: To represent bondage

From the Minor Arcana

* Eight of Swords: To represent being tied up and constrained
* Ten of Swords: To represent being pinned down

The Hanged Man Card Spell

Take a picture of your target, with eyes showing, and name it. Then state that the person is suspended from harming you. Glue the picture of the target to the Hanged Man card. Punch a hole at the top and thread string through it. Then tie this someplace high, such as a ceiling fan or a tree, and leave it there to hang for an indefinite amount of time.

The Devil Card Spell

This card depicts a man and a woman in bondage. If your target is male, glue a picture of the target's face over the man's face, and if the target is female, do the same but over the woman's face. Name the picture and state that due to all of the target's wrongdoings, the person is now in bondage by the devil and can no longer harm anyone. Bury the card in a cemetery.

The Eight of Swords Card Spell

As stated earlier, this card depicts a person bound and tied to a fence or cage of swords. Glue the face of the target to the face on the card. Name the card and tell the target that they are binded from harming you. Find a deserted wooden fence or one that is not in view of people. The front of the card will face the fence. Anoint the heads of nine coffin nails, then pound them through the card and into the fence.

The Ten of Swords Card Spell

Obtain a picture of your target, with eyes showing, then name it. Tell the target that they are pinned down and no longer able to cause you further harm. Place the card atop the picture so that the back of the picture is facing a pincushion. Then push thirteen pins through the card and picture and into the cushion to secure it in place.

Enslaving with Effigies: The Doll-Babies

An effigy is any image or representation of a person. For centuries, our ancestors have successfully used effigies in spellwork. The most common effigies utilized by rootworkers are doll-babies—also called poppets or voodoo dolls by other traditions.

The popular cloth dolls vary in size and can be easily made or purchased, but dolls can also be created from materials such as bread dough, clay, meat, mud, paper, or anything that can be shaped to resemble your target. In the following chapter on cursing and hexing your enemies, I will teach you how to make various type of dolls. However, prepurchased plastic dolls, the tiny Guatemalan worry dolls, and stuffed toys, such as teddy bears or monkeys, will work nicely for binding purposes.

Stuff the Doll

Insert name papers, petition papers, the target's pictures, and/or any personal concerns into the doll. Usually, the head of a plastic doll can be removed from the body. If only the head is hollow, it will suffice for the filling. For stuffed dolls, make incisions into both the head and the body to insert the concerns. Sometimes, it is necessary to remove a portion of the manufacturer's stuffing to accommodate the supplement, which is perfectly acceptable. Then repair the incisions by sewing them back together.

Baptize and Name the Effigy

Baptizing and naming an effigy is performed to bring an essence of the target's spirit into the effigy or confirm representation of the target. My preferred method is similar to how Catholic priests do it: anoint your second and middle fingers with Holy Water or Florida Water, then with those two fingers, make the sign of the cross over the crown of its head while stating aloud: "I baptize you in the name of the Father, of the Son, and of the Holy Spirit, Amen."

Next, hold the effigy up toward the ceiling or sky with both of your hands while picturing volts of electricity running up your arms and into the image while stating aloud: "And I name you (target's name)." Repeat the target's name for a total of nine times while screaming the name on the ninth time.

Now, hold the effigy in front of your face and state: "I now give you the breath of life." Place your mouth over the mouth of the image and blow air into it. The effigy is now ready for spellwork.

Contain the Cop

My client's grandson was a fourteen-year-old genius, and we both had hopes of him growing up to be president of the United States. Instead, he used his talents for robberies, drug dealing, and scams. At that early age, he led a double life, fooling his grandmother into believing he was a studious child while running with a gang. He was also the mastermind for the group's ingenious strategies and victories, which his grandmother later discovered in written diaries as diagrams and plots.

She wondered why the police had not yet uncovered his wrongdoings. My readings revealed he was also engaged in magical practices. She vehemently denied his knowledge of spellcraft until she discovered a teddy bear, dressed as a police officer, that was bound and blindfolded. She sent it to me, and I disassembled it. The teddy bear had a name paper of the police precinct's captain. The outside of the doll had been frequently sprayed with salt water, as I could see the residual dried salt. Yes, the kid was truly a genius! Sadly, once the spirit was released from the doll, the child was immediately caught for a scroll of illegal offenses and ultimately served a long jail sentence. Nevertheless, here is the spell to avoid the police:

Buy a stuffed animal and insert the name paper and photograph of the presiding police sergeant or captain of the nearby squadron into it. Dress the toy as a police officer. Name it, baptize it, and command it to be blinded to your affairs. Cover its eyes with a blindfold and tie its hands behind its back. On a daily basis, spray it with salt water while commanding that this official and those under their authority remain helpless in discovering your undertakings and identity.

Dominate the Dummy

Prepare a plastic doll by stuffing it with the petition paper, personal concerns, and knotweed. Name it, baptize it, and command that it be binded from harming you. With duct tape, cover its mouth and bind its appendages.

Keep it in the bathroom on paper towels. Whenever you have to urinate, place the doll under the stream of your urine while stating that the target is binded and under your domination. Return the doll to the paper towels and replace the paper towels regularly to avoid the rancid odor of stale urine.

The doll will retain the stench of stale urine. So when that odor eventually becomes unbearable, take it outside and affix it to something stationary to keep the target binded.

Gag the Gossip

Buy a stuffed animal. Although I prefer monkeys for gossipers, a teddy bear is fine. Stuff it with the name paper and a photograph of the culprit. Make another incision into the mouth and stuff this with a petition paper to stop gossip, and add a generously large amount of alum. If slippery elm is available, add that too. Sew the mouth shut. Baptize it, name it, and command it to stop gossiping. Then wrap a lot of duct tape around the mouth.

Place it somewhere that you can easily see it, laugh at it, and command it. On a daily basis, spray it with alum dissolved in warm water while commanding that the target stop gossiping.

The Spiderweb Snare

Spiderwebs and old spiderwebs such as cobwebs are sticky materials designed to immobilize their victims. If using a newer spiderweb, please ensure that it has been abandoned by the spider.

Buy a small Guatemalan worry doll or a slightly larger cloth doll. Stuff it with the name paper and petition paper. Name and baptize it. Then, entangle the doll with, or into, the web while demanding that it bind the target from committing further harmful acts against you. For larger dolls, you may perform other binding spells, or place it in a box containing knotweed, then seal it.

The Twine Tie-Up

Prepare a material-made doll by stuffing it with the petition paper, personal concerns, and, if desired, knotweed. Name it, baptize it, and command that it be binded from harming you.

Anoint the heads of nine coffin nails with Controlling/Domination Oil, and with them, nail the doll close to an area with twining vines. I use my own railings outside in order for the morning glories to twine around them. Some people will nail the doll near poison ivy, but if you do so, please wear gloves and protective clothing to avoid contamination by the ivy.

Rock Repression

Prepare a material-made doll by cleansing and stuffing it with the petition paper, personal concerns, and, if desired, knotweed. Name it, baptize it, and command that it be binded from harming you.

Ask the permission of the spirit of a large rock for assistance in binding the target from further harm to you. Wait a few minutes for a feeling of approval or disapproval. If you are granted permission, anoint the top of a large and heavy rock with Controlling/Domination Oil. Lay permanent bonding glue on the front of the doll and place it underneath the rock while stating that the target is permanently binded from harming you. Thank the spirit of the rock.

Magnet Mania

Prepare a material-made doll by stuffing it with the petition paper, personal concerns, knotweed, and a strong magnet. Name it, baptize it, and command that it be binded from harming you.

Place this in a small metal box. The magnets in the doll will bind the target to the box. Before closing the lid, anoint the inside of it with Controlling/Domination Oil.

Snap Trap Suppression

Prepare a material-made doll by stuffing it with the petition paper, personal concerns, and, if desired, knotweed. Name it, baptize it, and command that it be binded from harming you.

Obtain a snap mousetrap, which is inexpensively sold in packages of three in dollar stores. While telling the doll that it is trapped from committing further harm to you, cautiously lift the metal bar, place an appendage of the doll underneath it and release the bar to entrap it. Talk to the doll on a daily basis, while laughing at it because it is as weak as a mouse.

Freezer Spells

Freezers and blocks of ice are used to assist in binding. Freezer spells are employed to freeze and thus bind a person out of one's life. They are also effective in freezing an undesired anticipated or ongoing behavior or activity, such as testifying in court, making trouble on the job, gossiping, or interfering with familial or romantic relationships.

Always remember that anything placed in the freezer that contains names, images, or personal concerns will be frozen out of your life. Therefore, never write out your own name, the place of your employment, or that of anyone important to you. For example, if your love interest is John, but Jane is interfering, only Jane's name, image, or personal concerns would be placed in the freezer. If you tried to freeze out their relationship by putting both of their names in the freezer, then he too would be frozen out of your life.

This rule also applies to the preservation of a personal concern that contains the fluid, such as semen, vaginal secretions, blood, or urine of a loved one. Once it is in the freezer, that person will be frozen out of your life.

Also, when writing out a petition, avoid what I like to call "a grocery list"—meaning that there are too many commands or unnecessary verbiage that will result in confusion. The petition ought to be simple and straight to the point. Many clients have asked me if the use of such terms as *me, my,* or *I* is acceptable. The answer is *no!* First, the wording goes straight to *your* essence, and second, it alerts me to the fact that the client is attempting to write a grocery list. Thus, if I wanted Steve out of my workplace, I would simply write out his name for a freezer spell. If I had access to his images or personal concerns, they too would be included.

There's one common mistake that people often make that yields consequences: performing freezer spells on groups of people. For example, if I wanted four people out of my workplace and wrote out the names of Steve, Jane, John, and Mary, the spell may work by removing me from the job, thus manifesting my desire to freeze them out of my life. Therefore, to avoid this type of manifestation, only work on one person at a time and start with the ringleader of the group.

Do not attempt to freeze out the next person until the first person has departed.

Yes, working on one person at a time is a tedious process, but being fast and sloppy will yield fast and sloppy outcomes. Keeping your spells simple will provide favorable manifestations. Look at the webpage "20 Inspirational Quotes on Simplicity" by Habits For Wellbeing. There are many famous people such as Albert Einstein, Steve Jobs, and others who have spoken on the beauty of simplicity. My favorite quote is from Hans Hofmann who said:

> *The ability to simplify means to eliminate the unnecessary so that the necessary may speak.*

Bind and Freeze

Obtain a picture of the target, with eyes showing, and name it. Place some knotweed on the photo. Wrap it in black yarn, but start off by leaving a tail in order to tie knots at the end of the spell. Continue to entwine the image while continuously saying aloud: "(Target's name), I bind you from causing further harm to me." Keep wrapping it until the picture is completely enclosed in the yarn. Tie nine knots. Immerse the ball in water, then set it in aluminum foil with the shiny side facing the ball. Wrap it up in the foil and set it in the freezer.

Cow's Tongue Freezer Spell to Stop Gossip

Aluminum foil, a generous amount to ensure that there's enough to completely wrap the tongue

Beef tongue

Razor blade, or other sharp cutting tools

Picture of the target, with eyes showing

Powdered alum

Slippery elm

Personal concerns of the target, if available

Vinegar

Large sewing needle

Black thread

9 coffin nails

Spread out a large piece of aluminum foil, shiny side up, and place the beef tongue on it. With a razor blade or other sharp cutting tool, carefully making a deep slit over, but not through, the tongue. Start at the thinner side of the tongue and continue making the slit about six inches toward the thicker side—this will obviously be done horizontally.

Take the picture and write the target's name over it nine times, but do not write over the eyes. Turn it to the left and cross it with the command *Shut up* nine times. Place a generous amount of alum powder and slippery elm over the picture and command the person to shut up and stop gossiping.

Now fold it once away from you. Turn it to the left and fold it away from you again and set this in the center of the cut tongue. Add the personal concerns, if available.

Place more powdered alum and slippery elm over the contents now inside the tongue. Pour vinegar over it. Sew it shut with the thread and needle. Pound nine coffin nails into the tongue. Wrap it up tightly with the aluminum foil and place it in the freezer.

Hypothermic Hysteria

Create a small doll representing your target. Name and baptize it. Fill an oblong plastic container that has a lid a quarter of the way full of water and a binding ingredient. Put your doll in the water and place it in the freezer. The doll will float to the top, but it will remain stationary in the water as long as it stays frozen. Cover the doll and ice with enough water to submerge the doll, and secure the lid on the container. Return the container to the freezer.

The Old "Peepsicle Spell"

Write out the name of the target and put it in a container. Place a rock over it to hold it down, because water will try to force it to float to the top. Now, add enough water to fill the container two-thirds full. If the person is a gossiper, add Stop Gossip Water. Do not fill the container to the top as water expands when frozen. Place a lid on the container, wrap it in a black cloth, and set it in the freezer. This spell does take time to manifest but yields great results.

Mirror Madness

Who's the Ugliest of Them All?

Tape a picture of your target, with eyes showing, to a mirror. Ensure that the image is facing the mirror and state that all the evil that is in the target will bounce back to that person.

Compact Cruelty

Moisten your middle and index fingers with your own urine. Draw the sign of an *X* over a picture of your target, with eyes showing. State that the target is now confined and under your control. Place the picture in a brand-new mirror compact, without gazing into your reflection, with the target's image facing the mirror. Close the compact and use duct tape to seal it. Do not reopen the box as the cumulative evil energies will escape, return to its owner, and reenergize the target.

Mirror Box Binding Spell

This is a pretty safe spell to perform because whatever the target is will bounce back to them. So if this is a good person, then no harm will befall them. But if the target has an evil nature, those monstrosities will bounce right back. The freezer will ensure that the target will be binded to their own wrongdoings.

You will need six small, two-inch or four-inch mirrors, and duct tape. Do not catch your gaze with the mirrors. With two strips of duct tape, sticky side up, make a cross on a flat surface to form the foundation. Lay one mirror, shiny side up, in the middle of the cross of the tape. From there lay one mirror, shiny side up at each side of the first mirror. Bring each mirror up, along with the duct tape until you've formed five sides of a box. Place a picture of the target inside the box and command: "Whatever you are will bounce back to you and stay with you." Complete the box by topping it off with the last mirror facing inward.

Then wrap a generous amount of duct tape all around the box, ensuring that no cracks are visible. Then set the mirror box in the freezer.

Spells for Justified Cursing and Hexing of Your Enemies

Cursing, crossing, or hexing is the act of placing a magical spell on another with the intent to cause harm. In Hoodoo and Conjure, there are many terms for the same intentions including:

* Crossing
* Jinxing
* Messing someone up
* Throwing (or throwing shade)
* Tricking

You might also hear an elderly person refer to someone who is the victim of a curse as having been *rooted*, *goofered*, or *hurt*. Although there are numerous terms to define curses or types of curses, for the sake of simplicity, the terms in this book will be kept to a minimum.

Seek Revenge or Walk Away?

Often, people forget about malicious intent directed toward them. Instead they decide that life is too precious, as well as too short, to waste their time seeking revenge on their offenders.

However, there are many who cannot forget or forgive the pain and anguish that had been imposed on them and will therefore demand justice. Whether you decide to walk away or seek magical revenge, do what feels right for you.

If the decision has been made to seek magical revenge, keep in mind that it *must* be justified! Also remember to ensure that you, your home, and your loved ones, such as children and pets, are protected. Without protection, the energies associated with negative spells can also attach themselves to those who do not have protection in place. Additionally, you must also ensure that you have spiritually cleansed both yourself and your home after the spells have been executed, and those instructions will be provided in the last chapter.

Most importantly, wait for your revenge. Allowing time to elapse is good for two reasons:

1. It provides for excellent planning.

2. The enemy is off guard.

Plan Your Spiritual Attacks As If You Were a Military General

Sun Tzu was a successful military general and strategist who lived around 500 BCE. He wrote one of the most important military dissertations entitled *The Art of War*. His essay remains the most influential strategic text in East Asian warfare while influencing both Eastern and Western military thinking, as well as business and legal tactics!

In the chapter called "Laying Plans," General Sun Tzu said: "When able to attack, we must seem unable; when using our forces, we must seem inactive; when we are near, we must make the enemy believe we are far away. . . ." Later in the chapter he writes: "Attack him when he is unprepared, appear where you are not expected."

What does this all mean? Act submissive, walk away from any altercations, appear weak and helpless, and keep out of your enemy's sight and thoughts. Then start your warfare when the enemy's guard is down. This is especially important in spiritual warfare because if your enemy suspects magical retaliation, they may set up spiritual protection to guard against any possibilities of an attack.

Sometimes it may take a while to execute your plans, so your patience will be challenged. But time is actually on your side because it allows you to observe the enemy's habits and weaknesses, which provides the spellcaster more opportunities to exact justice. As with the old adage, "Revenge is a dish best served cold," a cool and calm disposition in the planning phase will give you the chance to create a calculated strategy.

Beneficial Times to Utilize Intense Emotions

Have you ever said to yourself: "I am so angry that it makes my blood boil"? There is some truth to that expression because when humans are enraged, our heart rates and blood pressure increase, causing amassed tension within the body that's ready to erupt like an explosion. There might be visible signs of unreleased tension such as teeth grinding, fists clenching, sweating, flushing, and so on.

Therefore, immediately following an initial assault is the perfect time to release that anger in spoken words or, if you're like me, screaming words! As we have previously discussed, sound is energy, frequency, and vibration, and, most importantly, sound is power. When releasing tension through sharing it aloud, those words are overflowing with power. Instead of wasting that precious energy with nonsensical and useless profanities, state or scream your desired outcome for the enemy out loud, and be precise in your commands. Walk away from the altercation, then scream something like "(Target's name), you will lose everything that's important to you!"

The second beneficial time to do this is when you are actually performing your spells. Remind yourself of the triggering events and rejuvenate your anger before speaking your cursing commands. Now, on to the business of cursing and hexing . . .

Man-Made Tools Commonly Used in Cursing and Hexing Spells

It is traditional to use physical items to torture an image of your enemy. Below are some suggestions for cursing tools, but don't feel limited to this list. Be creative and use your ingenuity to select anything that you believe to be a useful instrument.

* Barbecue grill
* Baseball bat
* Boiling water
* Broken glass
* Chains
* Coffin nails
* Frying pan
* Hammer
* Hot oil
* Ice pick
* Knife
* Lighter or matches
* Mousetraps
* Nails or tacks

* Needles
* Nets
* Pins
* Rat poison pellets
* Razor blades
* Rope
* Rust
* Saw
* Soldering iron
* Staples
* String, thread, or yarn (preferably black)
* Wires

And although they are not man-made, two other effective items to use are large and heavy rocks and stones taken from a location that has experienced a severe tragedy.

Stones or Dirt from Catastrophic Events

On September 11, 2001, a terrorist attack was staged against the Twin Towers in New York City. Two airplanes crashed into the towers, resulting in the death of 2,996 people and the injury of 6,000 others. It was the deadliest terrorist attack on American soil. Unfortunately, my new boyfriend gave me a stone from the debris of that attack.

That stone turned out to be emitting profuse amounts of negative vibrations that affected everybody in my home. There was constant screaming, arguments, confusion, and feelings of profound desperation and impending doom—emotions that I have never experienced in my life.

Stones or dirt that has withstood devastating events, such as that stone given to me, will absorb and retain that negative energy. Because their spirits cannot permanently contain such a vast amount of negativity they will, in turn, emit those energies. Thus, they are great sources to add in your cursing and hexing spells.

Herbs and Minerals Used for Cursing and Hexing

It is advisable to use gloves while handling these plants because some of them, such as henbane, are toxic. Additionally, plants with needles, such as cactus thorns, sweet gum, and especially the superfine needles of pica-pica pods, can penetrate the skin.

If you are making powders from some of the ingredients listed on the following page, the herbs and minerals ought to be finely crushed and blessed before their use in spellwork.

Once finely crushed, they can be placed on a charcoal disk and utilized as incense.

* **Asafoetida** (*Ferula-assa foetida*)
* **Bitter root, dogbane** (*Apocynum androsaemifolium*)
* **Bittersweet** (*Celastrus scandens*)
* **Black or brown mustard seeds** (*Brassica nigra, Brassica juncea*)
* **Black pepper** (*Piper nigrum*)
* **Black salt** (sodium chloride, carbon, and *Piper nigrum*)
* **Black walnut leaves** (*Juglans nigra*)
* **Blueberry** (*Vaccinium frondosum*)
* **Cactus thorns** (Cactaceae family)
* **Celandine** (*Chelidonium majus*)
* **Charcoal** (carbon)
* **Chicory** (*Cichorium intybus*)
* **Couch grass, dog grass** (*Agropyron repens*)
* **Cruel Man of the Woods** (*Strobilomyces floccopus*)
* **Henbane** (*Hyoscyamus niger*)
* **Peanuts, peanut shells, peanut leaves** (*Arachis hypogaea*)
* **Pica-pica or velvet bean** (*Mucuna pruriens*)
* **Poppy seeds** (Papaveroideae subfamily)
* **Red pepper** (*Capsicum annuum*)
* **Saltpeter** (potassium nitrate)
* **Skunk cabbage** (*Symplocarpus foetidus*)
* **Snake head, balmony** (*Chelone glabra*)
* **Spanish moss** (*Tillandsia usneoides*)
* **Sweetgum** (*Liquidamber orientalis*)

* Volcanic ash *(tephra)*
* White salt *(sodium chloride)*

How to Make Black Salt

Also known as Witches' Salt, this is commonly used for cursing. To make your own, mix white salt with scrapings of a charcoal disk or charcoal briquette and some black pepper.

Animal and Insect Curios Used for Cursing and Hexing

Please do not cause pain, suffering, or torment to any living being nor engage in unnecessary plant, insect, or animal sacrifices. Every organism has a right to life. Use the ones that have already died naturally or purchase them already deceased.

Again, a gentle reminder to consider the nature of the animal or insect when implementing them in spellwork. For example, quite a few people I knew are erroneously stuffing cursing candles with deceased cicadas. Throughout time, in various myths and folklore, cicadas represent both carefree living and immortality. Cicadas are therefore an inappropriate curio to utilize in negative spellwork.

On the other hand, flies and maggots are usually found around feces and rotting organic materials, and it is therefore their nature to represent waste and decay. Additionally, as has already been stated, excrement from animals that have a horrific stench, such as that of dogs, are used rather than the sweet-tasting cat feces (which dogs love to eat)! Here are examples of what could be implemented in negative spellwork:

* Ants
* Cockroaches

* Dirt dauber nest
* Dog feces
* Dog vomitus
* Flies
* Maggots
* Rats
* Rat feces
* Scorpions
* Snakes and their byproducts
* Spiders
* Wasps

Powders, Oils, and Washes for Cursing and Hexing

There are numerous quality condition powders, oils, and washes on the market for your purposes. You may choose to leave it to the experts by purchasing the products or be creative and make your own by using the aforementioned lists as a guide. However, some products, such as Pica-Pica Powder, ought to be purchased rather than homemade, because of the pod's fine, sticky needles.

Powders

From the specified lists of herbs, minerals, or animal curios for cursing and hexing, be creative and make your own powders. Any powder made from herbs or minerals can be converted into an incense by placing it on a charcoal disc.

Listed on the following page are the most commonly used powders in the Hoodoo or Santería traditions. They are most often found in contact magic but not to be used as an incense.

Graveyard dirt: For the purposes of cursing and hexing, this dirt ought to be acquired from the gravesites of a criminal, or several criminals, who committed heinous crimes. Acquire the dirt as described in the last chapter.

Goofer Dust: Derived from the Kilongo word *kufwa,* meaning "to die," the original formula contained toxic poisons. As time passed, the recipes have been modified and vary from one practitioner to another. Mine is to mix equal amounts of powdered snake sheds or snakeskin with gunpowder, black salt, and cayenne pepper. Add this mixture to a larger amount of graveyard dirt then combine. If desired, you could also add powdered dog feces and/or rat feces to the mixture.

Pica-Pica Powder: Also known as "itching powder" it is sold in most Latin spiritual stores or botanicas.

War Powder: Made from the rust of iron. Simply scrape the rust off any iron object to create the powder. If desired, add cayenne pepper.

Oils and Sprays

Confusion Oil
Both celandine and poppy seeds cause confusion, and both are available as oils. Placing poppy seeds in celandine oil or celandine in poppy seed oil makes great formulas for causing your target to experience cruel confusion.

Disgust Oil
Place several dead spiders, flies, and/or maggots in four ounces of mineral oil. Put the cap on the bottle, shake well, and set in in a dark area for a month. It is now ready for use.

Creating Sorrow Oil

Blueberry causes sorrow and chicory adds strength to any curse. You will need:

2 ounces almond oil

2 drops vitamin E oil (serves as a preservative)

1 drop blueberry essential oil

Small pieces of chicory root

Add all ingredients to a glass bottle, then recite a blessing prayer over the formula. Secure the cap on the bottle, shake vigorously, and set it in a dark cool area. Then shake daily for two weeks. Your oil is now ready for use.

Creating Sorrow Spray

Bring three cups of water to a rapid boil, then remove the pot from the heat. Place blueberry leaves and chicory root in the water and allow these plants to steep for thirteen minutes. Strain the mixture and keep the water. Respectfully place the plants outside on the ground from whence they came. When the liquid has cooled, pour it into a spray bottle and keep it refrigerated until ready for use.

Making Your Own Cursing and Hexing Oil

Black pepper, frequently used in cursing spells, is available as an essential oil. This will be the foundation for your cursing oil, along with the almond carrier oil and the vitamin E oil used as a preservative. Thereafter, add whatever ingredients that are available to you. The recipe would look like this:

2 ounces almond oil

2 drops vitamin E oil (serves as a preservative)

1 drop black pepper essential oil

Small pieces of red peppers, red pepper flakes, a pinch of salt, bitter root, black mustard seeds, pieces of skunk cabbage, and/ or any of the herbs or minerals used for cursing and hexing.

Snake sheds, optional

Place all of your ingredients in a glass bottle, then recite a blessing prayer over the formula. Secure the cap on the bottle, shake vigorously, and set it in a dark cool area. Then shake daily for two weeks. Your oil is now ready for use.

Cursing with Prayers

There are several psalms that contain, or are meant to inflict, curses—including Psalms 35, 58, 137, and, the harshest of them all, Psalm 109. Be advised that even when reciting holy texts that call upon God to justifiably inflict harm upon your enemies, it will nevertheless draw the attention of curious malevolent entities.

Therefore, ensure that both your body and the space around you are protected, as discussed in chapter 2, before reciting any of these. Remember to pray the psalms aloud and, before closing the prayers with *Amen,* tell God the entire story and ask for justice. Do not ask for the type of justice; God will make that decision. As stated in the Bible, Romans 12:19; "for it is written, **Vengeance is mine;** I will repay, saith the Lord."

Whichever psalm you choose to recite, do so on at least three consecutive days at around the same time each day or night. But, out of respect for God, do not recite them on the day of the Sabbath. In Judaism, this falls from a Friday at sundown to Saturday at sundown. In Christianity, it falls on a Sunday. Therefore, since I have no idea which should take precedence, I recommend reciting them consecutively on Tuesdays, Wednesdays, and Thursdays while avoiding both the Judaic and Christian Sabbaths.

PSALM 35 (KJV)

1 Plead my cause, O LORD, with them that strive with me: fight against them that fight against me.

2 Take hold of shield and buckler, and stand up for mine help.

3 Draw out also the spear, and stop the way against them that persecute me: say unto my soul, I am thy salvation.

4 Let them be confounded and put to shame that seek after my soul: let them be turned back and brought to confusion that devise my hurt.

5 Let them be as chaff before the wind: and let the angel of the LORD chase them.

6 Let their way be dark and slippery: and let the angel of the LORD persecute them.

7 For without cause have they hid for me their net in a pit, which without cause they have digged for my soul.

8 Let destruction come upon him at unawares; and let his net that he hath hid catch himself: into that very destruction let him fall.

9 And my soul shall be joyful in the LORD: it shall rejoice in his salvation.

10 All my bones shall say, LORD, who is like unto thee, which deliverest the poor from him that is too strong for him, yea, the poor and the needy from him that spoileth him?

11 False witnesses did rise up; they laid to my charge things that I knew not.

12 They rewarded me evil for good to the spoiling of my soul.

13 But as for me, when they were sick, my clothing was sackcloth: I humbled my soul with fasting; and my prayer returned into mine own bosom.

14 I behaved myself as though he had been my friend or brother: I bowed down heavily, as one that mourneth for his mother.

15 But in mine adversity they rejoiced, and gathered themselves together: yea, the abjects gathered themselves together against me, and I knew it not; they did tear me, and ceased not:

16 With hypocritical mockers in feasts, they gnashed upon me with their teeth.

17 Lord, how long wilt thou look on? rescue my soul from their destructions, my darling from the lions.

18 I will give thee thanks in the great congregation: I will praise thee among much people.

19 Let not them that are mine enemies wrongfully rejoice over me: neither let them wink with the eye that hate me without a cause.

20 For they speak not peace: but they devise deceitful matters against them that are quiet in the land.

21 Yea, they opened their mouth wide against me, and said, Aha, aha, our eye hath seen it.

22 This thou hast seen, O LORD: keep not silence: O Lord, be not far from me.

23 Stir up thyself, and awake to my judgment, even unto my cause, my God and my Lord.

24 Judge me, O LORD my God, according to thy righteousness; and let them not rejoice over me.

25 Let them not say in their hearts, Ah, so would we have it: let them not say, We have swallowed him up.

26 Let them be ashamed and brought to confusion together that rejoice at mine hurt: let them be clothed with shame and dishonour that magnify themselves against me.

27 Let them shout for joy, and be glad, that favour my righteous cause: yea, let them say continually, Let the LORD be magnified, which hath pleasure in the prosperity of his servant.

28 And my tongue shall speak of thy righteousness and of thy praise all the day long.

PSALM 58 (KJV)

1 Do ye indeed speak righteousness, O congregation? do ye judge uprightly, O ye sons of men?

2 Yea, in heart ye work wickedness; ye weigh the violence of your hands in the earth.

3 The wicked are estranged from the womb: they go astray as soon as they be born, speaking lies.

4 Their poison is like the poison of a serpent: they are like the deaf adder that stoppeth her ear;

5 Which will not hearken to the voice of charmers, charming never so wisely.

6 Break their teeth, O God, in their mouth: break out the great teeth of the young lions, O Lord.

7 Let them melt away as waters which run continually: when he bendeth his bow to shoot his arrows, let them be as cut in pieces.

8 As a snail which melteth, let every one of them pass away: like the untimely birth of a woman, that they may not see the sun.

9 Before your pots can feel the thorns, he shall take them away as with a whirlwind, both living, and in his wrath.

10 The righteous shall rejoice when he seeth the vengeance: he shall wash his feet in the blood of the wicked.

11 So that a man shall say, Verily there is a reward for the righteous: verily he is a God that judgeth in the earth.

PSALM 137 (KJV)

1 By the rivers of Babylon, there we sat down, yea, we wept, when we remembered Zion.

2 We hanged our harps upon the willows in the midst thereof.

3 For there they that carried us away captive required of us a song; and they that wasted us required of us mirth, saying, Sing us one of the songs of Zion.

4 How shall we sing the Lord's song in a strange land?

5 If I forget thee, O Jerusalem, let my right hand forget her cunning.

6 If I do not remember thee, let my tongue cleave to the roof of my mouth; if I prefer not Jerusalem above my chief joy.

7 Remember, O Lord, the children of Edom in the day of Jerusalem; who said, Rase it, rase it, even to the foundation thereof.

8 O daughter of Babylon, who art to be destroyed; happy shall he be, that rewardeth thee as thou hast served us.

9 Happy shall he be, that taketh and dasheth thy little ones against the stones.

PSALM 109 (KJV)

1 Hold not thy peace, O God of my praise;

2 For the mouth of the wicked and the mouth of the deceitful are opened against me: they have spoken against me with a lying tongue.

3 They compassed me about also with words of hatred; and fought against me without a cause.

4 For my love they are my adversaries: but I give myself unto prayer.

5 And they have rewarded me evil for good, and hatred for my love.

6 Set thou a wicked man over him: and let Satan stand at his right hand.

7 When he shall be judged, let him be condemned: and let his prayer become sin.

8 Let his days be few; and let another take his office.

9 Let his children be fatherless, and his wife a widow.

10 Let his children be continually vagabonds, and beg: let them seek their bread also out of their desolate places.

11 Let the extortioner catch all that he hath; and let the strangers spoil his labour.

12 Let there be none to extend mercy unto him: neither let there be any to favour his fatherless children.

13 Let his posterity be cut off; and in the generation following let their name be blotted out.

14 Let the iniquity of his fathers be remembered with the Lord; and let not the sin of his mother be blotted out.

15 Let them be before the Lord continually, that he may cut off the memory of them from the earth.

16 Because that he remembered not to shew mercy, but persecuted the poor and needy man, that he might even slay the broken in heart.

17 As he loved cursing, so let it come unto him: as he delighted not in blessing, so let it be far from him.

18 As he clothed himself with cursing like as with his garment, so let it come into his bowels like water, and like oil into his bones.

*19 Let it be unto him as the garment which cov-
ereth him, and for a girdle wherewith he is girded
continually.*

*20 Let this be the reward of mine adversaries from the
Lord, and of them that speak evil against my soul.*

*21 But do thou for me, O God the Lord, for thy name's
sake: because thy mercy is good, deliver thou me.*

*22 For I am poor and needy, and my heart is
wounded within me.*

*23 I am gone like the shadow when it declineth: I am
tossed up and down as the locust.*

*24 My knees are weak through fasting; and my flesh
faileth of fatness.*

*25 I became also a reproach unto them: when they
looked upon me they shaked their heads.*

*26 Help me, O Lord my God: O save me according to
thy mercy:*

*27 That they may know that this is thy hand; that
thou, Lord, hast done it.*

*28 Let them curse, but bless thou: when they arise, let
them be ashamed; but let thy servant rejoice.*

*29 Let mine adversaries be clothed with shame, and
let them cover themselves with their own confusion,
as with a mantle.*

*30 I will greatly praise the Lord with my mouth; yea,
I will praise him among the multitude.*

*31 For he shall stand at the right hand of the poor, to
save him from those that condemn his soul.*

The Cursing Spells

Ancient Cursing Spells

Thousands of years ago, our ancient ancestors implemented several types of cursing spells that involved casting the evil eye, cursing dolls—both to be discussed later in this chapter—and other types of magic such as curse tablets and binding spells. A conspicuous aspect of ancient spellcasting is the prevalent basic principles of the past are virtually identical to those upheld to this day. In the book *Curse Tablets and Binding Spells from the Ancient World,* researcher and author John G. Gager discovered that the three prevalent practices of the ancients included:

1. Verbal declarations or commands.

2. Appealing prayers to supernatural forces for assistance.

3. Analogies in which the target takes on the characteristics of the tools used in the spells.

These tools would include dolls, curse tablets, and other objects. Here are two examples of such spells.

The Lead Curse Tablet

Lead is cold, heavy, and poisonous. Therefore, inscriptions on pieces of lead that had been discovered by archeologists were often inscribed with words such as: "As this lead is cold and useless, so may: (target's name) be cold and useless!" These tablets would then be dropped into springs, wells, or other locations in which the tablets would sink.

Pottery Punishment

The ancients often inscribed the name of their target onto pottery. Then that pottery would be smashed into pieces, symbolizing the abolishment of their target's power. In other parts of the world, the pottery would be smashed in a temple, serving a twofold purpose: the ear-piercing sound of the crashing pottery would draw the attention of the entity being summoned for assistance while disempowering their enemy.

In the practice of Hoodoo, Santería, and other magical belief systems, it is held that there is an entity, or path of an entity, that resides at the crossroads. He is often referred to as "The Man at the Crossroads." Later in this book, you will learn that an option for the deployment of ritual items will include a verbal command immediately followed by the disposing, or smashing, of items at a crossroad. Therefore, it has always been my personal contention that this practice, just as in ancient times, is for the purpose of attracting his attention to obtain assistance.

For in-depth insights into the importance of Jewish magical spellwork of the ancients, I highly recommend the book *Sepher Ha-Razim: The Book of Mysteries,* translated into English by Michael A. Morgan. This work discusses the realms of where the holy angels reside, as well as their duties, the summoning incantations, and the actual spellwork. Implemented together, the cursing spells can invoke hair-raising afflictions upon an enemy.

Bottle Bane Spells

Container spells are one of my personal favorites because they are designed to confine the essence of the enemy alongside the undesirable contents of the bottle or container. Depending on your intention, these spells can inflict nightmares or invoke bizarre behavioral changes for the target.

Alcoholic Anguish

If the target is a frequent consumer of alcohol, keep him drunk and confused. Obtain a photo of the target, with eyes showing. Name and baptize it, then command that they will remain drunk and confused. Pour whiskey into a glass bottle, and add a generous amount of poppy seeds and mix well. Then place the image of the target into the bottle and seal it with a lid. Keep the container in a cool, dark, isolated area and leave it alone.

Decomposition Distress

Do not, under any circumstances, kill an animal for this spell. Instead, make use of an animal that has already died. Ask the spirit of the animal to assist you with the spell and explain what the target has done to you. If you feel a sense of consent from the animal's spirit, then perform this spell.

Insert something representing your target—such as a doll, a picture, a name paper, or personal concern—into an open container. Place a dead rat, snake, or other small animal over the representation of the enemy. State aloud that as this animal's body decays, so too will the happiness of (target's name). Keep the container outside and a distance away from children or pets. Once the animal has completely decomposed, empty the contents of the container into a sewer.

Dog Doom

When people's dogs defecate on my lawn, it pleases me because dog feces are a great cursing ingredient. Dog feces have a foul odor and attract flies that deposit maggot eggs, as well as other disgusting organisms. Place the feces in an open container, preferably a clay pot, outside. Insert something representing your target such as a doll, a picture, a name paper, or personal concern in the feces. State aloud that as these feces stink and attract foul elements, so will (target's name). Water the feces every day to prevent them from drying out and to nurture the maggots.

Female Frenzy

This spell is designed to make a woman sexually undesirable. Take an open container, preferably a clay pot, outside.

Empty the contents of cans containing anchovies, sardines, and/or snails into the pot. Then insert something representing your target such as a doll, a picture, a name paper, or personal concern into the pot and stir well. State aloud that as this fish rots and stinks and attracts foul elements so will the vagina of (target's name).

Halloween Horror

My Godparents in Santería frequently told me that if I cannot find revolting dead animals or insects, then I should use my imagination. During the Halloween season, when disgusting plastic creatures are readily available, my Godparents would have me purchase several bags of small plastic or rubber spiders, tarantulas, worms, skeletal bones, and the like along with other creepy insects to place in a glass jar as a representative of the creatures. However, the jars must be jam-packed with these creepy toys while the image of your target in the lower middle of the jar is entrapped by them. In other words, surround the image with the toys. After a few days, spray everything with poisonous insect killer.

Obviously, the toys won't be harmed, but the fumes may take effect on the target's aura. Keep the bottle sealed and outside along with spraying the creatures outdoors. Believe it or not, I have seen this spell work in the form of nightmares, and sometimes the target will feel as if something is crawling on them or will experience intense itching.

Inevitable Insanity

Rip a large piece from a brown paper bag, avoiding the factory cuts or stamp marks. Lay it flat and sprinkle some of the target's personal concerns or foot track dirt over it. Sprinkle a generous amount of poppy seeds over the personal concerns, followed by black dog and cat hair, and finally, gunpowder. Wrap this up tightly as you state aloud that your target will go insane, then place it in a small bottle. Seal the lid and throw the bottle in a river, running stream, or sewer.

Insatiable Insomnia

This spell is most often performed on a mate or a family member. Place both a dead spider and dead fly in a small black box. Tell their spirits what the target has done to you and ask them for assistance with your spell to cause the person insomnia. Slip this under the target's pillow while you state aloud that this person will have persistent problems sleeping.

Smoky Sorrow

This spell was given to me by a beloved elder who is no longer alive. It was pointed out to me that liquid smoke, in large quantities, is a carcinogen. Hot sauce, on the other hand, contains vast amounts of liquified pepper, which is a common cursing ingredient. Both can be purchased at any grocery store. Empty the contents of both bottles into a larger glass bottle or jar with any personal concerns and mix well. Insert something representing your target such as a picture, name paper, or doll in the bottle.

Place a lid on the bottle, and for thirteen days, shake the bottle vigorously as you state your curses aloud. Then bury the bottle near a tree or in a cemetery.

Candle Cursing

There is usually enough space on a figural candle to inscribe the target's name, crossed over with your command. This can be performed several times over smooth surface areas. On the other hand, only the command is inscribed on a taper candle either three, nine, or thirteen times, depending on its length.

The inscribed commands must complement the intent of your spellwork. For instance, if John Doe had tormented me, then my justified revenge would be to inflict torment in return. Thus, the command "torment" would be inscribed on the candle, as well as on the petition paper. Examples of common cursing commands may include, but are not limited to, the following:

* Bewilderment
* Chaos
* Confusion
* Damnation
* Destruction
* Distress
* Horror
* Illness

* Insanity
* Insomnia
* Mayhem
* Nightmares
* Sorrow
* Torment
* Trauma

Take notice that the *death* command was not included on this list. Remember that the curse must be proportionate to the crime. If you're reading this book, you're obviously not dead, so a death spell is not justified. If the enemy caused death to a loved one, then a death command might be something to consider. However, it is not recommended because, if manifested, it will indeed provide immediately gratification but could sadly be followed by serious and permanent psychological or spiritual consequences.

There are hundreds, if not thousands, of candle cursing spells, and all spiritual practitioners have their own creative and cunning preferences. The following are just some of my favorites.

Confusing Cell Block

Aluminum cookie sheet

Coasters

13 petition papers

13 candleholders

13 black 4-inch or 6-inch candles

Confusion oil

Poppy seeds

A representation of your target such as a doll or effigy, picture, or personal concern

Place the aluminum cookie sheet on the coasters. Prepare and anoint each individual petition paper and fold them, as described in chapter 2, and place them in the candleholders.

If using four-inch candles, inscribe the word *confusion* three times on each candle. The six-inch candle has enough surface area to inscribe the command nine times, whereas a jumbo candle can easily be inscribed thirteen times.

Trim the candle wick to avoid lengths that interfere with the spellwork, Now, anoint your candles with the oil, roll them in poppy seeds, and immediately place them in the candleholders.

Place the representation of your target in the middle of the cookie sheet and also anoint it with confusion oil. Place four of the 4-inch candles at the square cardinal points surrounding the enemy's representation.

Set the other nine candles in a square pattern, enclosing both the image as well as the first four candles in order to represent prison bars within prison bars.

Light the candles and scream your command aloud. You could state something like: "(Target's name), you are isolated, alone, and confused. You can't think straight. You're mentally ill!" Do this several times during the combustible time of the candles. You don't have to remain with them constantly, but they need to be checked frequently.

Whenever you enter the area near this altar, repeat your commands. Remember, screaming is a form of emitting energy that quickly disperses into the universe. Get mad!

Get angry! Get loud! Get your intent communicated effectively to the spirit world!

Extinguishing the candles for this spell is not recommended because it interrupts the momentum and execution of the spell. When the candles have extinguished themselves, wrap up the petition papers, candle wax, and representation of the target in a black cloth and place this in a dark black box in your freezer.

Candle Jar Spell for Sorrowful Idiots

Sorrow Oil

Personal concerns of the target and/or pictures with eyes showing

Petition paper

32-ounce jar with a metal lid (without manufacturer's markings on the lid)

4 ounces white vinegar

4 ounces spoiled milk

9 coffin nails

9 pins

9 needles

3 pica-pica pods

1 tablespoon poppy seeds

1 tablespoon red pepper flakes

1 tablespoon goofer dust

1 tablespoon graveyard dirt

1 tablespoon black mustard seeds

Broken glass

Small tube of gelled glue (e.g., Gorilla Glue, Crazy Glue)

8 black, 6-inch taper candles

Begin this spell on a Tuesday or Saturday night of a waning moon. With a pencil, inscribe the candles from top to bottom in spiral fashion with the word *sorrowful* for a total of nine times (try not to lift the pencil). Anoint the candles with the oil from top to bottom. The petition paper can be crossed with the word *sorrowful* and anointed.

Place the personal concerns and the petition paper inside the jar. Put everything else except the glue and candles in the jar. The jar ought to be two-thirds full. Do not fill it higher because both the vinegar and spoiled milk contain gases that can explode the jar. State your curse as many times as possible.

Before placing the lid on the bottle, smear the glue on the inside lip of the lid (or the threads of the jar). This is to prevent the gases from the milk and vinegar forcing the lid off. Secure the lid on tightly, and shake the jar vigorously.

This spell does not require a candleholder. Hold a match under the bottom of one of the candles until some wax has dripped onto the lid. Then firmly place the candle on the melted wax and let it harden. Check for candle stability before lighting it.

Once the candle is lit, recite your prayers and petitions aloud. This is a six-hour candle; therefore, it will help to repeat your prayers and petitions at least once more during the six-hour period. Once the candle has been consumed, remove the wax remains and throw them at a crossroad.

Repeat this spell every Tuesday and Saturday of the waning moon. Since there are normally two Tuesdays and two Saturdays a month that fall on a waning moon phase, the spell will take two months to perform.

During the waxing moon phases keep the jar in a sealed freezer bag to avoid leakage. On any day of the week, shake the jar vigorously, keeping it in the sealed bag, while screaming your curses.

Once the waning moon returns, remove the jar from the bag to continue the candle work. Once the eighth candle has been consumed, smash the jar at a crossroad while again screaming your curse. Walk away and do not turn around to look back because that would be symbolic of distrusting the work. Do not return to that area.

Erectile Dysfunction Candle Spell

Saltpeter causes impotence and is an effective ingredient for negative spellwork. This is a great cursing spell for rapists or cheating men.

½ teaspoon saltpeter

2 ounces warm water

Small spray bottle

1 Black Penis figural candle

Picture of the target (optional)

Metal or aluminum pie plate or cookie sheet

Coasters

9 rusty nails, coffin nails, pins, or needles

First, mix the saltpeter with the warm water inside your spray bottle and set aside.

Inscribe the target's name and birth date on the candle. Name and baptize it, then inscribe the word *impotence* all over the candle for a total of either nine or thirteen times. If a picture is used, write the word *impotence* over the forehead.

Set the pie plate or cookie sheet on the coasters. Place the picture of the target, with the image facing upward, on the plate or sheet. Heat the tips of the nails, pins, or needles one by one and stick them into the penis candle at various areas over the candle, then set this over the picture. Spray the entire candle and picture with the dissolved saltpeter.

Once the liquid has dried, light the candle and state your curses aloud.

Once the candle has been consumed, the wax remains will most likely be abundant. Not to worry, just throw the wax remains, pins, needles, or nails, along with the image, into the sewer.

Skull Candles

The initial appearance of these candles may convey the notion that they are meant for evil or Satanic purposes, but this is an unadulterated misperception. Skull candles represent the human brain, which can easily be manipulated to change a person's attitude or behaviors. I have implemented these candles, thousands of times, for spellwork involving matters of love, courage, sorrow, remorse, forgiveness, and especially breakup and cursing magic, while enjoying successful results for both myself and my clients.

Hundreds of my neophyte clients have also enjoyed successful results through my magical coaching. They were willing to invest the work involved to be victorious and took the time to understand the human brain and what it controls. It's not that difficult, and I will explain these areas in simple terms.

What Is the Human Brain?

The Mayfieldclinic.com describes it as "an amazing three-pound organ that controls all functions of the body, interprets information from the outside world, and embodies the essence of the mind and soul. Intelligence, creativity, emotion, and memory are a few of the many things governed by the brain. . . ."

The human brain is divided into four main lobes, which are what we manipulate in spellwork. Take a look at what the lobes control, then find the areas in the illustration on page 180.

The Functions of the Brain Lobes

The information below is supplied by the Mayfieldclinic.com:

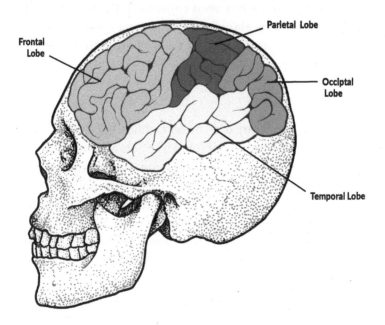

Frontal Lobe

* Personality, behaviors, emotions
* Judgment, planning, problem-solving
* Speech: speaking and writing
* Body movement
* Intelligence, concentration, self-awareness

Parietal Lobe

* Interprets language, words
* Sense of touch, pain, temperature
* Interpret signals from vision, hearing, motor, sensory, and memory

Occipital Lobe

* Interprets vision (color, light, movement)

Temporal Lobe

* Understanding language
* Memory
* Hearing
* Sequencing and organization

Examples of How to Manipulate the Brain

Sight: If your desire is for the target to see certain things, then place those images in both the eyes and the occipital lobes as well as into the parietal lobes.

Thoughts, speech, or behaviors: To manipulate the target's thought processes or to control their behaviors, insert petition papers or ingredients into the frontal lobe.

Inflicting pain: Probe needles, pins, nails, etc., into the parietal lobes.

Hearing: The temporal lobe and the ear are the locations to influence your target.

Items Needed for Skull Candle Spells

First and foremost, skull candles ought to be stuffed with petition papers, ingredients, and/or images. This is extremely difficult, if not impossible, to do with small candles. Therefore, I do not recommend using a skull candle smaller than four inches in height and seven inches in diameter. Then you will need:

Skull candle

Soldering iron (do not use inside the home)

Pencil

½ by ½-inch pieces of torn brown paper bag for petitions

Cursing oils

A small funnel

Personal concerns of the target

Cursing herbs and minerals

A syringe or spoon to refill the skull candle

A melted chime candle of the same color as the skull candle

Metal pie plate

Coasters

Picture of the target, with eyes showing

Preparing the Skull Candle

Step 1. Cleanse the candle.

Step 2. Because of the toxic fumes emitted, always use a soldering iron outdoors. Bore holes into the areas of the candle you wish to manipulate. The frontal lobe is always an area I utilize for any type of skull candle spell.

Step 3. With you pencil, write one-word commands on the petition papers, anoint them with oil, then roll them up and stuff them into the areas of the candle that you wish to control.

Step 4. With your funnel, place any personal concerns of the target and the cursing ingredients into the bored holes.

Step 5. Refill the holes, one at a time, with the melted wax. Wait until the wax has completely hardened, which takes about four minutes, before sealing the next hole.

Step 6. With your pencil, inscribe the target's name and birth date on the candle.

Step 7. Name and baptize the candle.

Step 8. Inscribe cursing commands all over the candle, paying close attention to the lobes that correlate with the commands.

Step 9. Anoint the candle with the oil and sprinkle cursing herbs and/or minerals, if desired.

Step 10. Set the pie plate over the coasters. Then place a picture of the target on the pie plate, image facing upward, and set the candle directly over the picture.

Step 11. You are now ready to begin any of the following candle spells.

Fire Safety Reminders

Never use large petition papers inside any figural candle as they will create bonfires once ignited. Check on any ignited candle frequently to ensure that the flame is under your control. It is also a good idea to cover the altar with sand before placing the coasters and metal plate on it. If you must leave your home, snuff out the flame. Never leave a lit candle unattended.

Interpreting Skull Candle Wax Remains

There are certain behaviors that a skull candle will exhibit that cannot be represented in symbology books. Some candle wax symbology correlates with the lobes of the brain and may include:

* **Inside of skull candle is consumed:** You have psychologically impacted the target, but if other areas remains intact, there is resistance.

* **The entire face falls off:** The target may understand the situation but is unwilling to face it or the spell command.

* **The forehead and face remain intact:** This the frontal lobe of the brain indicating resistance from the target

who is unwilling to believe the spell suggestion or to obey a command.

* **The back of the head remains intact:** This is the occipital lobe area that controls vision and indicates resistance from the target who is unwilling to see what has been shown to him.

* **A side of the head remains intact:** The temporal lobe remains intact indicating the target is unwilling to listen to any of the spell commands.

* **The candle melts completely but leaves a puddle of wax:** This suggests great progress but not completion. Additional spells need to be performed.

* **The picture underneath the candle burns:** This indicates success.

Skull Candle Spells

Let Me Go Crazy on You!
This spell will influence the target to be enraged, confused, and physically restless. Everything the target says will also be confusing and delivered in a heated manner.

1 skull candle

Hot Foot Oil (see recipe in the chapter to send enemies away)

Poppy seeds

Cayenne pepper

Volcanic ash, to cause explosive anger

Target's personal concerns

Five ½-inch by ½-inch command papers that say *insanity*

Prepare your candle as previously instructed. With your soldering iron, bore holes into the mouth as well as into the frontal, parietal, and temporal lobes.

Anoint your command papers with the oil and insert them into the lobes. Mix equal amounts of poppy seeds, cayenne pepper, and volcanic ash and insert the mixture into the mouth as well as the lobes, keeping a little aside to sprinkle over the candle. Add personal concerns. Seal the holes with wax.

Anoint the candle with a generous amount of oil and sprinkle the remaining poppy seeds, pepper, and ash mixture over its entirety.

Light the candle. Every hour on the hour while the candle remains a viable image of a skull, go to the left temporal side of the candle and scream into the ear and temporal lobe: "You are going crazy!" Then scream and laugh nonsensically as if you are insane. Do this three times.

Go to frontal lobe and repeat this process, then to the right temporal lobe, and, finally to the occipital lobe where you will scream the command four times, which will total thirteen times.

When the flame extinguishes itself, read the candle remains and throw them into a river, running stream, or sewer.

Prickling Pica-Pica

I once stood under a tree, and somehow an ant got into my hair. It was an agonizing experience because, even after having applied antilice medication as well as washing my hair tens of times, my imagination got the best of me and the sensation of it crawling all over my head persisted. It made me feel disgusting. It wasn't until days later that my physician checked me out and saw nothing. That's when the disgusting crawling and itching sensations finally subsided! Here's a spell to do the same to your enemy.

1 skull candle

Disgust oil

Dead ants

Target's personal concerns

Pica-Pica Powder

Three ½ by ½-inch command papers that say *it itches*

Prepare your candle as previously instructed. With your soldering iron, bore holes into the frontal and parietal lobes.

Anoint your command papers with the oil and insert them into the lobes along with the dead ants and personal concerns. Seal the holes with wax. Anoint the candle with a generous amount of oil and roll the candle in Pica-Pica Powder.

Light the candle. Every hour on the hour while the candle remains a viable image of a skull, go to the left temporal side of the candle and scratch yourself while stating that the target has an unbearable itching sensation everywhere. Say something like: "You have uncontrollable itching. It just won't stop itching. You feel dirty." Do this three times. Go to the frontal lobe and repeat this process, then to the right temporal lobe, and finally, to the occipital lobe where you will recite the command four times, which will total thirteen times.

When the flame extinguishes itself, read the candle remains but do not throw the wax in any body of water as it could alleviate the itching. Instead, bury the remains near a tree, in the woods, in the cemetery, or in the target's pathway.

Teasing Torture

This candle does not require burning. It is a great effigy to torment each and every time you are reminded of the torment that was caused to you.

1 skull candle

Cursing oil

Goofer Dust

Target's personal concerns

Six ½ by ½-inch command papers that say *tortured*

Duct tape

Prepare your candle as previously instructed. With your soldering iron, bore holes into the frontal, occipital, and both of the temporal and parietal lobes.

Anoint your command papers with the oil and insert them into the lobes along with the Goofer Dust and personal concerns. Seal the holes with wax. Place duct tape around the candle to cover its eyes. Then anoint the candle with a generous amount of oil and roll the candle in Goofer Dust.

Keep the candle outside, away from animals and children. Each and every time you feel anger, scream your curses aloud while kicking, stabbing, burning, poking, or slicing it. If there is bad weather, ensure that the candle is exposed to it. A torridly hot day is especially nice because it will partially melt the effigy.

This spell can be performed indefinitely. However, once you no longer feel the desire to work with it, wrap it up completely with a black cloth. Then generously use duct tape to wrap the candle until it is completely encased within the tape. Beat it with a baseball bat or a hammer every day until it no longer takes the form of a skull. Then throw it in a river, stream, or sewer.

Useless Vagina Repugnancy

Alum has a puckering effect by drawing out moisture and pulling soft tissue together. Cuban botanicas used to sell chunks of alum to young women who wished to trick their mates into believing they are virgins. On their wedding days they would temporarily insert a chunk of alum into their vaginal canals right before engaging in sexual intercourse.

Because alum causes tissue closure, it is one of the main ingredients in this spell and useful against promiscuous women who are sleeping with your mate.

1 vagina candle

Powdered alum

1 can of anchovies in oil

A ½ by ½-inch command paper that says *repugnant*

Target's personal concerns and/or picture

Because of the horrific odor the ingredients will emit, it is advisable to perform the spell outside. Cleanse the candle. Inscribe the target's name and birth date on it, then name and bless it. Inscribe the words *useless* and *repugnant* all over the candle.

With your soldering iron, bore a hole into the vaginal opening and insert the command paper, powdered alum and, if available, your target's personal concerns. Seal the hole with melted wax.

Anoint the candle with the anchovy oil. Place the candle over a picture of your target, image facing upward, then surround the base of the candle with the anchovies. Allow this to sit in an isolated area for two days.

Remove the anchovies; place them in a small plastic bag and set aside. Light the candle and recite your prayers, curses, and commands. Once the candle has extinguished itself, place the wax remains in the plastic bag containing the anchovies. Seal the bag and put it in your freezer to freeze her vagina for further activities.

Contact Cursing Magic (Laying Tricks)

As we discussed in chapter 4, these types of spells involve the target either having direct contact with a bewitched item, such as touching or stepping on it, or indirect contact, including walking over the item, being near the item, or just passing by it.

When preparing the trick, ensure that the intention is clearly stated, including stating the enemy's name and the desired manifestation. Visualizing the desired calamity is essential.

Most importantly, always remember that after the trick has been laid, just walk away without turning or looking back. Doing so demonstrates a lack of confidence in your spells as well as a lack of faith in your spiritual court.

The Goofer Ball Trick

There are two ways of making trick balls. One is with wax and the other with papier-mâché. The hard-wax balls are not permeable to water and will not disintegrate. It is the preferred choice if your target will most likely pick them up. Papier-mâché, on the other hand, will disintegrate when exposed to water, such as rain, causing the tricking ingredient to disperse, providing a larger area and greater chance for the target to step over the trick.

To make wax balls, melt two black chime candles in a small metal container. As the wax begins to cool, remove the floating wicks, and stir into it one tablespoon of Goofer Dust. Check the temperature of the wax with your fingers to ensure that it is not too hot. Once cooled enough to form balls, do so while verbalizing your petition. When the balls have completely hardened, throw them into your target's yard where they will likely step on them or touch them.

To make papier-mâché balls, slightly moisten the mixture and combine it with the Goofer Dust. Form the balls and set them aside for a day or two to allow them to harden.

The Goofered Gift of Duration

Buy a pretty little stuffed animal, such as a teddy bear. With a sharp cutting tool, make fine slits into the toy and insert Goofer Dust. Then sew them up.

If you have access to a syringe and a large gauge needle, rather than cutting the toy you could instead inject the toy. Dissolve Goofer Dust in warm water, then aspirate the formula with your syringe and inject the solution into various areas of the toy.

Send the gift anonymously with a beautiful card in order to deceive the target into believing that it is from an anonymous admirer.

The Gravely Handshake

Rub your hands with graveyard dirt from a deceased person who had suffered. Shake hands with the target or touch them. Immediately wash your hands with Florida Water or a water and sea salt mixture.

Two Peanut Pranks

Peanuts have been utilized in cursing spells for centuries in Hoodoo, Santería, and Palo. When I became a palera, I was warned never to eat peanuts as it will weaken my powers. These spells are from the book *Folk Beliefs of the Southern Negro* by Newbell Niles Puckett, PhD.

Bad Luck: To cause bad luck, throw peanut hulls on your enemy's doorstep.

Car Trouble: Drop peanuts on the floor of your target's automobile, as this will cause the car to break down.

Problematic Pica-Pica

This is a common curse relayed to me by several babalawos, the high priests of Santería. If someone is creating problems for you in the workplace, return the favor! Pica-Pica Powder causes problems for a target who comes into contact with it. Place some of the powder in your hand, state your curse, and blow it into the workstation of your enemy. Immediately wash your hands with Florida Water or a water and sea salt mixture.

Doll Dilemmas

For thousands of years, people have been making dolls to represent their targets using whatever materials are accessible that will form an image of the person. Commonly called doll-babies, voodoo dolls, and poppets, depending on the faith of the practitioner, they are created in order for the practitioner to assert dominance over their target, as in cursing and hexing spells, or to persuade a person to do their bidding in both negative as well as love work.

Doll-babies can be made from any material that can be molded such as:

* Bread dough
* Butter
* Clay
* Ground meat
* Mud
* Play dough
* Wax

They can also be fashioned out of anything that will create a likeness of a human figure which could include, but is not limited to:

* Cloth
* Metals (the ancients' common method)
* Toy dolls, stuffed toy animals
* Twigs

Numerous spellcasters make exquisite looking dolls, and their remarkable creative talents could leave the impression that dolls must be fashioned by highly experienced people. This is not the case. Personally, I lack any artistic qualities and struggle just to draw a reasonable looking stickman. All my clay dolls look like they could be from another planet, yet they work beautifully. Am I envious of all the spellcasters who possess phenomenal artistic talents? Of course! But, in the end, all that really matters is that my dolls are effective.

Obviously, they must be fashioned to resemble the target, as it is essential for the spellcaster to effectively visualize the enemy's image. Inserting the target's personal concerns, or taglocks, into the effigy creates the magical link, while naming and baptizing the doll summons an essence of that person's spirit into your tool.

If personal concerns are not available, the doll can still be effective. However, the chances of manifestation are much weaker. I have had success using merely name papers and photographs. So, if personal concerns are not available, don't be discouraged. Take a gamble—you have nothing to lose and you might have a lot to gain!

Butter Doll-Baby

More than a century ago, when slaves were forced to churn butter, they would steal a bit for themselves to eat or to craft dolls of the slave masters. This simple, yet effective, spell is one of many that slaves and old-time Hoodoo practitioners implemented.

Expose a tub of whipped butter at room temperature until the butter has warmed. Craft the butter to resemble your target. If you have personal concerns, insert them into the doll. If the butter becomes too warm, cool it in the refrigerator for a few minutes. Remove it from the refrigerator, then carve the target's name and birth date onto it. Name and baptize it.

You can either burn the doll in a frying pan or set it outside to melt under the hot sun.

Crafting and Working a Clay Doll-Baby

When crafting clay dolls, it is essential to use air-drying clay. Never bake your dolls because heat not only changes the composition of personal concerns and cursing ingredients, but it will also kill the spirits within the herbs and minerals.

1 package air-drying clay

1 vat of warm water

1 roll paper towels

Pencil

Petition papers

Personal concerns of your target

Photograph of your target (if available)

Cursing ingredients

Cursing oils

Divide the packet of clay into three sections: one for the back torso; one for the front torso; one for the legs, arms, penis if male, and head. Place these sections in the warm water to prevent rapid drying.

Place layers of paper towels on a flat surface to absorb the moisture of the clay absorbed from the warm water. Ensure that each section of the clay is molded over fresh paper towels.

Remove one section of the clay from the water to make the back portion of the torso. This will be the foundation of the doll. Knead it flat until there is enough clay surface to contain the personal concerns and the cursing ingredients. With your pencil, inscribe the target's name and birth date into the clay.

With the second section of the clay, mold out the two limbs and head and press all of these pieces into the foundation. Next, set the personal concerns, petition papers, name papers, cursing ingredients, oils, and photograph over the foundation portion of the doll.

Knead the last section of the clay to make the top torso portion, but ensure that it is just slightly smaller than the bottom portion. Inscribe the targets, name and birth date on this portion also. Then lay it over the foundational clay to completely cover the limbs and ingredients. Fold the foundation portion up and over the top section and mold the entire doll until there are no visible seams.

The drying period becomes a little time-consuming. It does require that the doll rest on fresh layers of paper towels daily and be turned at least once a day until it is completely dry.

Cursing a Clay Doll-Baby

Once the doll has dried, as with any doll, name and baptize it. Always maintain direct eye contact with the doll and uphold an authoritative and commanding tone of voice.

While remembering the pain that the enemy has caused, you could burn it with a lighter, matches, soldering iron, or even a barbecue grill, while you scream your curses. But do not get the doll wet as the clay will soften. Do not urinate or spit on the doll as it will absorb your taglock into it.

Keep the doll stored in noxious materials such as a cloth sprayed with insect repellent or one that contains dog feces or dried up vomitus.

Crafting and Working a Cloth Doll-Baby

Here are two easy ways to craft a cloth doll.

Cloth Doll 1. Acquire either a black or white cloth. However, if it is an article of clothing that the target has worn, then the color is not as relevant because it contains taglocks such as dried skin cells. Ensure that the side of the cloth containing the taglocks faces inward.

Patterns for dolls can be found online that simply resemble a gingerbread cookie man. Because of their simplicity, they can be hand-sewn. Sew one side closed and work with the open side.

Stuff the doll with as many personal concerns as possible. Add one or more petition papers, small pictures of the target, and name papers. Then put in cursing ingredients. If the contents seem sparse, add Spanish moss for extra filling Then sew the doll shut.

Cloth Doll 2. Purchase a craft doll. Slit one side open, and remove the contents from the head and torso, leaving the limbs as they are. Fill the head with cursing ingredients. Insert the papers, personal concerns, pictures, and cursing ingredient into a small white crew sock or baby sock. Then place the sock in the torso section of the doll and sew it shut.

Cursing a Cloth Doll-Baby

With a black marker pen, draw an *X* where both eyes would be. Draw a circle over the mouth area to represent the target screaming in shock. Write the target's name and birth date on the back and the front torso. Then tie the hands behind its back.

Name and baptize it. Always maintain direct eye contact with the doll and uphold an authoritative and commanding tone of voice.

While remembering the pain that the enemy has caused, you can walk on it, bludgeon, kick, punch, or strangulate it. Hanging it by its neck from a tree limb and beating the doll with a baseball bat, as if it were a piñata, is also a common practice. Keep it exposed to harsh weather conditions. Do not urinate or spit on the doll as it will absorb your taglock.

Keep the doll stored in noxious materials such as a cloth sprayed with insect repellent or one that contains dog feces or dried up vomitus.

Meat Doll

Craft ground meat to resemble your target. If you have personal concerns, insert them into the doll along with a petition paper. Name and baptize the doll.

Take the doll to a park or wooded area and place it in isolation. State your curses over it and walk away. Whether a wild animal eats it or if it just rots away, the target will be negatively affected.

Twig Doll

This spell is to confuse and hot foot an enemy away. To make the head, fill a small piece of white or black cloth with poppy seeds and either personal concerns or name papers. Form it into a small ball and seal by either sewing or gluing the cloth. Then attach it to two twigs tied together.

At the opposite end, attach a chili pod to each twig, representing the feet. Name and baptize the doll and tell it to wander far away. Drop it off far from where the target resides.

The Evil Eye Curse

Whether it was because the US Air Force frequently exposed me to the sounds of gunshots and loud airplanes or being a daughter of the witch-path of Oshun who is hard of hearing, I am deaf in one ear. As a result of this, my voice is loud because I am unsure if others can hear me.

One day, at the library, the tone of my voice interfered with a man trying to read. He rose up, directly stared me in the eyes, and gave me a long, hard dirty look (and rightly so!). Then he departed. If looks could kill, I would have dropped dead that very moment! However, that stare lingered, making me nervous. After about ten minutes, I came to the realization that this man had inadvertently delivered the evil eye. I immediately washed away the curse with the Holy Water I always keep in my purse.

One can cast the evil eye out of anger, but it can also be delivered out of envy or jealousy. Have you ever been complimented by a smiling person, yet their eyes say otherwise? That's the evil eye! It can also be delivered through touch or verbalizations. If it ever happens to you, just spit three times on the ground while stating for the curse to be gone. If it happens to a beloved relative or pet, spit directly on them three times to remove the curse. Obviously I couldn't spit in the library, so spraying myself with Holy Water was another option.

But to deliver the evil eye, this is my method:

* Get as close as physically possible to the target.
* Stare directly into their eyes until you feel that you have reached their soul.
* Picture a black pool of ink surrounding their brain.
* Forcefully, but silently, repeat you commands several times, then walk away.

Penalizing Pictures

Seven Years of Bad Luck

For this spell, you will need either a two-inch or four-inch square mirror, a baptized and named picture of your target with eyes showing, and duct tape. Without catching your gaze in the mirror, place the picture atop the mirror with the image facing it. Duct tape it together. Throw it at a crossroad, and as soon as a car passes over it, the mirror will break causing the target bad luck.

Shoe Sins

Many cultures around the world insist that shoes must be removed before entering a person's home or a sacred place of worship, because both unknown microorganisms and negative spiritual energies attach themselves to the soles. Therefore, bringing shoes into the home also brings these undesirable conditions. Baptize and name a picture of your target, then glue it, with the image facing outward, to the bottom of your shoe. You are not only exposing the enemy to bacteria and negativity of the outside world, but also perpetually stomping on the target.

Doormat Dangers

Name and baptize a picture of your target, with eyes showing. Glue the back of the image to a doormat. Place a thin black cloth over the doormat and use glue at the edges to secure the cloth to the mat. Anytime visitors arrive, make sure they wipe their shoes on the doormat before entering. Leaving their shoes on the doormat is even better.

Variety of Viciousness

Here are a few ageless cursing spells from various parts of the world.

Fiery Feces

Burning an enemy's feces will cause severe constipation and, sometimes, even a bowel obstruction.

Hat Hatred

Mix graveyard dirt with powdered snake sheds. Dust this on the hat of your enemy to cause grave illness. Afterward, immediately wash your hands with Florida Water or a mixture of water and sea salt.

Plantain Persecution

Wrap the target's hair in a plantain leaf then bury it. This will cause your enemy to become physically ill.

Stabbing Shadows

From ancient to modern times, various cultures believe that people have an intimate relationship with their shadow. Therefore, stabbing the shadow of an enemy with a sharp object will cause grave illness. Kicking or walking over it will cause the target to feel restless.

Tree Trouble

To cause headaches, take the target's hair and stuff it into the groove of a tree's bark. Seal the groove with mud.

For more cursing and hexing spells, see my book *Cursing and Crossing: Hoodoo Spells to Torment, Jinx, and Take Revenge on Your Enemies.*

Spells to Justifiably Break Up Relationships

Simply defined, a relationship is a connection, association, or involvement of two or more concepts, objects, or people. One can participate in a relationship with not only a romantic partner but also family members, work associates, neighbors, clubs, places of worship, and other contexts.

An interpersonal relationship is a strong, deep, or close association between two or more people. These relationships fall into one of two categories—functional or dysfunctional. In a functional relationship there is a sense of stability, mutual respect, support, and security. Furthermore, the channels of communication are open. Dysfunctional relationships, by contrast, leave their victims with feelings of instability, ambiguity, tension, anger, or fear. The following are a few examples of dysfunctional interpersonal relationships and their sources.

* **Significant others:** Romantic relationships that have gone awry due to the interference of a third-party meddler.

* **Workplace:** Aggrieved employee-boss associations arising from the efforts of a hardworking and deserving

employee being ignored. Yet, another employee, who clearly exhibits substandard performances, receives favorable attention and accolades from their superior, due to their cunning and manipulative maneuvers.

* **Friends, neighbors, and other groups:** Inappropriate group dynamics in which there is a group leader, or instigator, showing malicious intentions toward others. Frequently, following the verbal or nonverbal cues of the leader, the group will persecute vulnerable people by delivering negative treatment or placing blame upon the innocent to inflict shame or create fear or flight feelings in the targeted individual.

So before becoming the victim of a dysfunctional relationship, it is imperative to recognize the warning signs. Many of my clients had suspected possible intruders, based on inappropriate behaviors or actions, but were unsure. So how can you tell if your relationship is in jeopardy or if it's just your imagination? First, always trust your gut instinct, because in almost all cases, it is either your own psychic intuition, a Spirit Guide, or your Guardian Angels trying to warn you. Then be attentive to warning signs that someone is indeed planning to steal your relationship. The following are just some of the most common signs, but there are many more:

Signs That Someone Is Trying to Steal Your Friends

* These people always want to hang out with your friends but never invite you to hang out with theirs.
* At group functions, you are avoided while your friends receive attention from the intruder.
* The intruder is overly amiable with your friends on social media.
* Your friends are invited, without you, to social events.

Signs That Someone Is Trying to Steal Your Job or Position

* A coworker is highly competitive.

* You are excluded from important e-mails or meetings.

* You are put on the defensive.

* They are repeat offenders, having stolen other jobs and positions in the past.

* The person becomes overly friendly, then tries to distract you from performing your job.

* The intruder will take credit for your work.

* Blame-placing is going on.

* Your faults are broadcasted.

* Rumors about you are broadcasted.

* A coworker is of equal rank but tries to present themself as your superior.

* They gossip a lot.

* The intruder tries to make you believe something about yourself or your boss that is untrue.

Signs That Someone Is Trying to Steal Your Partner

* There is constant communication with your partner through texting or social media.

* The intruder is affectionate with your partner, as well as overly attentive.

* If your partner believes they are being witty, the intruder laughs at everything being said.

* They gossip about you, plant seeds of doubt about you, and exploit your weaknesses.

* The intruder tries to talk and act like you. In other words, your personality traits are copied.

* The person always wants to hang out with your partner.

What do all these examples have in common? In each case, the culprit attempts to create dysfunction within an otherwise functional relationship with the goal of coercing their victim into total submission in order to remove the victim from their existing status. In other words, it is an attempt to break up a relationship to fulfill the offender's self-serving purposes.

Therefore, when an intruder begins to inappropriately and deliberately threaten the stability, respect, support system, and security that took blood, sweat, and tears to establish, it is time to turn the tables. Do unto them what they have done—or planned to do—unto you: break up the interpersonal relationship that is rightfully yours!

Please remember that breakup work is not justified for selfish purposes, such as desiring a person who is happy with another, stealing someone else's job or friends, or just to have fun. Taking someone or something that is not rightfully yours will create spiritual consequences. Again, allow me to remind you of God's words in the Holy Bible, Exodus 21:24–25:

Eye for eye, tooth for tooth, hand for hand, foot for foot,

Burning for burning, wound for wound, stripe for stripe . . .

In addition to spellwork, behaviors and thought processes must be modified. Otherwise, you may send one predator away but attract a new one. Consequently, you could ultimately find yourself in a never-ending battle. Always remember that your behaviors must complement your magic while your magic must complement your behaviors. In other words, they work hand in hand.

Modifying Your Behaviors

Why do some people fall victim to these types of predators more so than others? It's a three-word answer: trust and kindness. We want to see the good in others, but the "bad guys" view these behaviors as weaknesses. Thus, anyone with a pure soul can fall prey to their antics.

As stated earlier when we looked at sociopathic behaviors, some scientists believe that one out of every twenty-four people land in that category. Can you imagine being in a room with one hundred people and knowing that four to five of them are predators? Sadly, that's the ultimate reality of this generation.

Next, break those numbers down. There may be at least two to three predators in a room of fifty and at least one in a room of twenty-five. Therefore, you must always be aware that plenty of people have ulterior motives.

Predators can identify a vulnerable person within a few minutes. They look for body language signaling low self-esteem, such as slouching or hunching that makes the person look smaller and less assuming; fidgeting during conversations; or even nail biting. A predator will befriend these types of people, overly compliment them, and take steps to gain their trust.

They also look for people who smile a lot and display openness and kindness. Predators will present themselves to these types of people as victims in order to gain not only the target's sympathy but assistance as well. Thereafter, they continue to seek assistance and information for their own purposes. So be careful with your body language, and although it is honorable to be kind to others, trust others with caution.

No Lo Celebra!

Throughout my life, my Cuban mother would never allow me to brag over an accomplishment, possession, or new purchase. If I dared to boast about anything at all, she would interrupt by screaming, *"No lo celebra!"* In English it means "Don't brag."

Although my mother was more concerned about attracting the evil eye from others through jealousy, the hard reality is that others may try to physically take what you have. Therefore, it is a good policy to keep a low profile and avoid bragging about your accomplishments, job, partner, friends, and material possession to anyone, and especially on social media. Also avoid telling people your plans, ideas, and visions—a mistake I've made numerous times with pseudo-spiritual workers—because others can immediately take ownership of them and claim them as their own.

Even the Bible warns of bragging. As Psalm 75:4 of the New King James Version says, "I said to the boastful, 'Do not deal boastfully.'"

Never Underestimate People: A True Story

My medical education and work experience took years of hard labor to accomplish. I started as an Air Force aeromedical evacuation combat unit medic and instructor. Unfortunately, at the time of my enlistment, the G.I. Bill that pays for college education was not available due to the astronomical costs of keeping our troops in Vietnam.

Later, I wanted to attend college but could not afford it. I instead applied to a hospital-based licensed practical nurse (LPN) program, but they wanted all the money up front. So I worked two jobs, while also performing spiritual work, to save that money.

After becoming an LPN, my desire was to go on to be a registered nurse (RN). So I struggled by working full-time midnight shifts and attending college full time during the day. But LPNs didn't make a lot of money, so sacrifices had to be made.

First, the floor of my antiquated car had a huge hole I taped over with plastic bags. My classmates called it "The Fred Flintstone Car." During the winter, the slush from the mucky snow would dislodge the bags and completely dredge me with that ice-cold filth. Second, after paying for school, gas, rent, and utilities, there was rarely enough money left to eat, so when there wasn't time for spiritual work for a few extra dollars, I resorted to stealing crackers and ketchup in the cafeteria. Finally, the perseverance paid off and I became an RN and eventually earned a charge nurse position for a Level 1 trauma center.

Later, I managed to pay for my Bachelor of Science in nursing and finally my master's degree. But each degree required a full-time work and full-time college schedule all at once. It was a difficult task.

Finally, I made my way to hospital administration, which was the most stressful and psychologically challenging job I ever had. Nevertheless, not a bad accomplishment for an LPN with a Fred Flintstone car! It took eight years of formal education and more than fifteen years of hard work. Obviously, a lot of blood, sweat, and tears were invested to accomplish my goals.

After retirement, I returned to my roots of spiritual work and even sought further education in that venue. Later, I was contacted by a new client with minimal education and experience in spiritual work seeking the affections of a man.

Her educational history, she proclaimed, was a bachelor's degree in the arts. She consistently talked using very difficult words, and I found that behavior to be arrogant, fraudulent, and idiotic, because nobody talks like that. Nevertheless, she seemed desperate, and I felt bad for her.

As time went on, she successfully took advantage of my openness and kindness and positioned herself as a victim to gain my sympathy and assistance. I helped her with her spiritual classes and spellwork. The most peculiar aspect about her, however, was her continuous inquiries concerning my medical education and work résumé.

Underestimating her, I thought no harm could be done by telling her what she wanted to know again and again—after all, what could she possibly do with that information? Well, the answer is a lot! She acquired a traveling job teaching physicians about diabetes, which is a dream job for any master's degree–level nurse. Did she steal my résumé? It took me eight years of formal education and more than two decades of hard labor to be qualified for a job like that, yet she had cruised right into the position! Did she forge a nursing license too?

But wait, there's more! She became prominent in the spiritual world by parroting me, taking full credit for the spells I had developed, as well as copying and pasting my work on the internet and claiming it as her own. She took the concept of identity theft to a whole new level.

Although her actions did not personally hurt me—other than making me uncomfortable by her trying to be me—others will certainly be harmed. Her followers have no idea that she is a predator. Sadly, there are millions more just like her in this world.

What were my mistakes? I was too open, too kind, too giving, and too sympathetic. But my biggest blunder was underestimating her.

After you've read this narrative, it is my hope that you will review the signs of someone trying to steal your friends, job, position, or partner and compare those bullet points to my story. The knowledge will help you be prepared for any future hungry predators. Just remember to please be cautious with people you barely know and never underestimate them.

Now, on to the spellwork . . .

Priority One: Start by Sweetening the Target to You

Many times, neophyte practitioners will realize success-ful breakup spellwork, yet fail to achieve the favor of their desired target(s). Instead, that romantic partner, boss, or whomever they wished to win over will find a replace-ment for the one who has left, but in somebody else. This is because the practitioners neglected to first implant pos-itive thoughts about themselves in order to be favored. It is always a good idea to begin with a positive drawing spell, or sweetening spell, on the person(s) whose attention you wish to capture before initiating breakup spellwork. Hoodoo practitioners refer to these types of spells as "making a person sweet on you."

There are several types of sweetening spells. As the name implies, the practitioner would obviously work with ingre-dients containing sugar, fructose, glucose, sucrose, or other natural sweetening agents.

Throughout the years, it has been my observations that sweetening spells do not prompt actions. They do, however, encourage positive thoughts. Therefore, once the spellcaster has manifested this desire, it is recommended to continue the sweetening spells while introducing other spellwork to promote movement.

The easiest spell is to bind your picture with a picture of the desired target within a bowl of sugar, along with a petition paper. Although an effectively fast-acting spell, it is unfortunately not as stable or long-standing as those with viscous substances such as honey, sorghum syrup, or molasses.

My preference is a honey jar spell. Honey is slow acting, but it is also stable, long-lasting, and binding. Any type of honey will suffice, but I prefer working with orange blossom honey because both oranges and honey are favored by Oshun, the Santería orisha who rules the domain of love and money issues.

Honey Jar Spell

1 new glass jar with an unlettered metal lid

1 jar of honey

1 wallet-sized photo of your face with eyes showing

1 wallet-sized photo of target's face with eyes showing

2 strong magnets

White or pink yarn

Petition paper

Chime candles—pink for affection, blue for healing

Dried herbs that correlate to the condition (see below)

Herbs to Foster Friendship

Use a generous amount of one or more of the following:

* **Balm of Gilead, poplar buds** (*Populus candicans*)

* **Cloves** (*Caryophyllus aromaticus*)

* **Forget-me-not** (*Myosotis scorpioides*)

Herbs to Win Favoritism with Employers

Use a generous amount of one or more of the following:

* **Gravel root** (*Eupatorium puruream*)

* **Master of the Woods** (*Asperula odorata*)

* **Five finger grass** (cinquefoil)

Herbs for Reconciliation

Use a generous amount of one or more of the following:

* **Balm of Gilead, poplar buds** (*Populus candicans*)
* **Damiana** (*Turnera aphrodisiaca*)
* **Forget-me-not** (*Myosotis scorpioides*)
* **Spikenard** (*Aralia racemosa*)
* **Violet** (*Viola odorata*)
* **Rose petals** (*Rosa* spp.)

Fill the new jar halfway with honey, add the herbs, and stir with a wooden spoon or whatever tool is available. Add the petition paper and set this aside.

Dab a bit of honey, which also serves as a sweetening glue, on both images then stick the images together face-to-face. Place a magnet on either side to further bind the target to you.

Next, wrap this up with the yarn to create a ball. Start with a long tail hanging to be used for tying knots when the ball is completed. When creating this ball, state both the target's name and the intention for this person to have sweet and kind thoughts of you. When the ball is completed, leave extra yarn to create knots. Tie the tails together making either three, five, seven, or nine knots while repeating the intention each time that you tie a knot. Once this is completed, insert the ball deep into the honey jar.

Add more honey to fill the jar, replace the lid. On Mondays, Wednesday, and/or Fridays of the waxing moon, place a chime candle that has been anointed with either olive oil or a condition oil directly on the lid while praying or stating your petitions aloud. Continue this spell during the breakup work and afterward, to maintain ongoing sweet thoughts of you.

Herbs and Minerals Used to Break Up Relationships

* Black or brown mustard seeds (*Brassica nigra, Brassica juncea*)
* Black pepper (*Piper nigrum*)
* Black salt (sodium chloride, carbon, and *Piper nigrum*)
* Black walnuts (*Juglans nigra*)
* Celandine (*Chelidonium majus*)
* Charcoal (carbon)
* Couch grass, dog grass (*Agropyron repens*)
* Grains of Paradise (*Amomum granum-paradisi*)
* Lemon (*Citrus limon*)
* Lemon verbena (*Aloysia citriodora*)
* Peanuts, peanut shells, peanut leaves (*Arachis hypogaea*)
* Peonia, peronia (*Abrus hypogaea*)
* Pica-pica, velvet bean (*Mucuna pruriens*)
* Poppy seeds (*Papaveroideae*)
* Pumpkin (*Cucurbita* spp.)
* Red pepper (*Capsicum annum*)
* Volcanic ash (tephra)
* White salt (sodium chloride)

Animal and Insect Curios Used to Break Up Relationships

* Ants
* Black cat hair†
* Black dog hair†

---

† Please note that when using black dog and cat hair, do not use animals that live together or get along well. Do not use the hair of dogs that tolerate cats. Dogs and cats must be strangers to each other to encourage hatred and fights.

* Deer estrous
* Dirt dauber nest
* Dog feces
* Dog vomitus
* Human feces
* Human vomitus
* Human urine

Liquids Used to Break Up Relationships

* Habanero sauce
* Lemon juice
* Spoiled milk
* Vinegar
* War Water (for recipe, see pages 83–84)

Powders Used to Break Up Relationships

* Graveyard dirt
* Pica-Pica Powder

Making Your Own Breakup Oil, Powders, and Sprays

Breakup Oil

As with other negative spellwork, pepper and salt work well together. Black pepper is available as an essential oil. The foundation of your breakup oil will contain the black pepper essential oil, salt, black dog hair with black cat hair (to make them fight like cats and dogs), and vitamin E oil, which is used as a preservative.

Your foundation recipe would look like this:

2 ounces almond oil

2 drops vitamin E oil (as a preservative)

1 drop black pepper essential oil

A pinch of salt

A pinch of black dog hair

A pinch of black cat hair

Thereafter, add whatever ingredients are available to you from the list of herbs and minerals. My favored ingredients are a pinch of crumbled charcoal, cayenne pepper, crushed grains of paradise, and black or brown mustard seeds.

Place all of your ingredients in a glass bottle, then recite a blessing prayer over the formula. Secure the cap on the bottle, shake vigorously, and set it in a dark cool area. Then shake daily for two weeks. Your oil is now ready for use.

Breakup Powder 1

Mix equal amounts of the following ingredients:

Crushed black or brown mustard seeds

Crushed grains of paradise

Cayenne pepper

Salt

Breakup Powder 2

Mix equal amounts of the following ingredients:

Volcanic ash

Cayenne pepper

Salt

Breakup Spray

Boil eight ounces of water, then remove it from the heat. Immediately add half a teaspoon each of grains of paradise, black or brown mustard seeds, red pepper, black pepper, and salt. Allow the herbs to steep in the water for thirteen minutes, then strain. Respectfully lay the herbs outside on the ground and give gratitude for their lives.

Once the water has cooled, add the juice of one lemon and stir well. Pour this in a spray bottle and keep it refrigerated until ready for use.

Make Them Fall Out of Love Using Black Walnuts

Black walnuts are frequently used in Hoodoo spells to help people in doomed relationships overcome the love they had for their partners. In other words, it helps them to fall out of love with the one they have lost. However, black walnuts can also be used to make someone fall out of love with a partner that has been stolen from you.

Fall Out of Love Spray

With a hammer, crush three black walnuts in their husks into fine pieces. Put everything into a jar containing eight ounces of hot water. Secure the lid on the jar and shake well. Keep it at room temperature overnight.

The following day, place the jar in the refrigerator and shake it daily for seven days. After seven days, strain the mixture and pour the liquid into a spray bottle, then place it back in the refrigerator and use as needed. After fourteen days, the liquid will become rancid, so before this happens, pour it over a path the target will cross.

Fall Out of Love Powder

With a hammer, crush the meat of a black walnut until it is pulverized. Keep the powder in the freezer when not in use.

When ready to use, take the amount needed, and allow it to sit at room temperature for an hour before deploying it in your spellwork.

Prayers for Victory

When breaking up a relationship, it is my hope that you are doing so to reclaim what is rightfully yours. Thus, when a predator has interfered with your relationship or has gained possession of it, that person has sadly entered a battlefield in a war with you to the finish. Little does the enemy know that you have powerful backup troops: your spiritual court!

Remember to recite the prayers aloud and, before closing with *Amen*, tell the entity your entire story and ask for victory.

PSALM 59 (KJV)

1 Deliver me from mine enemies, O my God: defend me from them that rise up against me.

2 Deliver me from the workers of iniquity, and save me from bloody men.

3 For, lo, they lie in wait for my soul: the mighty are gathered against me; not for my transgression, nor for my sin, O Lord.

4 They run and prepare themselves without my fault: awake to help me, and behold.

5 Thou therefore, O Lord God of hosts, the God of Israel, awake to visit all the heathen: be not merciful to any wicked transgressors. Selah.

6 They return at evening: they make a noise like a dog, and go round about the city.

7 Behold, they belch out with their mouth: swords are in their lips: for who, say they, doth hear?

8 But thou, O LORD, shalt laugh at them; thou shalt have all the heathen in derision.

9 Because of his strength will I wait upon thee: for God is my defence.

10 The God of my mercy shall prevent me: God shall let me see my desire upon mine enemies.

11 Slay them not, lest my people forget: scatter them by thy power; and bring them down, O Lord our shield.

12 For the sin of their mouth and the words of their lips let them even be taken in their pride: and for cursing and lying which they speak.

13 Consume them in wrath, consume them, that they may not be: and let them know that God ruleth in Jacob unto the ends of the earth. Selah.

14 And at evening let them return; and let them make a noise like a dog, and go round about the city.

15 Let them wander up and down for meat, and grudge if they be not satisfied.

16 But I will sing of thy power; yea, I will sing aloud of thy mercy in the morning: for thou hast been my defence and refuge in the day of my trouble.

17 Unto thee, O my strength, will I sing: for God is my defence, and the God of my mercy.

PSALM 86 (KJV)

*1 Bow down thine ear, O LORD, hear me: for I am
poor and needy.*

*2 Preserve my soul; for I am holy: O thou my God,
save thy servant that trusteth in thee.*

3 Be merciful unto me, O Lord: for I cry unto thee daily.

*4 Rejoice the soul of thy servant: for unto thee,
O Lord, do I lift up my soul.*

*5 For thou, Lord, art good, and ready to forgive; and
plenteous in mercy unto all them that call upon thee.*

*6 Give ear, O LORD, unto my prayer; and attend to
the voice of my supplications.*

*7 In the day of my trouble I will call upon thee: for
thou wilt answer me.*

*8 Among the gods there is none like unto thee, O Lord;
neither are there any works like unto thy works.*

*9 All nations whom thou hast made shall come and
worship before thee, O Lord; and shall glorify thy name.*

*10 For thou art great, and doest wondrous things:
thou art God alone.*

*11 Teach me thy way, O LORD; I will walk in thy
truth: unite my heart to fear thy name.*

*12 I will praise thee, O Lord my God, with all my
heart: and I will glorify thy name for evermore.*

*13 For great is thy mercy toward me: and thou hast
delivered my soul from the lowest hell.*

> *14 O God, the proud are risen against me, and the assemblies of violent men have sought after my soul; and have not set thee before them.*
>
> *15 But thou, O Lord, art a God full of compassion, and gracious, long suffering, and plenteous in mercy and truth.*
>
> *16 O turn unto me, and have mercy upon me; give thy strength unto thy servant, and save the son of thine handmaid.*
>
> *17 Shew me a token for good; that they which hate me may see it, and be ashamed: because thou, LORD, hast holpen me, and comforted me.*

Saint Joan of Arc

Joan of Arc (1411–1431) was a victorious French military leader and warrior. During her lifetime, England, along with Burgundy, controlled most of France. At around age thirteen, Joan started receiving visions from Saint Michael the archangel and other spirits, urging her to help the true king of France reclaim his throne.

With the help of these deities, she led French troops from one victorious battle to another against England and Burgundy, until she brought Charles VII to the throne as the true French ruler. She herself died at the young age of twenty.

Saint Joan of Arc is often called upon to assist with victories in national wars or individual personal battles. Here is a beautiful prayer you can find posted on the website Daily Prayers:

PRAYER TO SAINT JOAN OF ARC

Saint Joan of Arc,

In the face of your enemies,

in the face of harassment, ridicule, and doubt,

you held firm in your faith.

Even in your abandonment,

alone and without friends,

you held firm in your faith.

Even as you faced your own mortality,

you held firm in your faith. I pray that I may be as bold in my beliefs as you, St. Joan.

I ask that you ride alongside me in my own battles.

Help me be mindful that what is worthwhile

can be won when I persist.

Help me hold firm in my faith.

Help me believe in my ability to act well and wisely. Amen.

If Your Situation Seems Hopeless

What if your partner is already walking out of the door or if that predator had already received the promotion that was rightfully yours? Well, it's never too late to pray for a miracle. Personally, I have seen hundreds of lost-cause cases miraculously turned around through the intercession of Saint Jude. After all, he is called "The Miraculous Saint" or "The Saint of Lost Causes."

Jesus Christ had two apostles named Judas. One was Judas Iscariot, who had betrayed Jesus and later killed himself, and the other was Judas Thaddeus, who is referred to as "Saint Jude" to not confuse him with the traitor. Many historians speculate that Saint Jude may have even been the brother of Jesus Christ!

Due to the confusion caused by two apostles named Judas, Saint Jude was widely ignored and ultimately forgotten for a long time. In order to be remembered, he later vowed to assist anyone who sought his help, especially those with the direst of problems, providing it wasn't of a harmful or illicit nature. The Catholic Church also wished to encourage his veneration and upheld the fact that he would indeed help anyone who felt that their problem was a lost cause. The following is a prayer to Saint Jude that is posted on the Catholic Online website:

PRAYER TO SAINT JUDE

St. Jude, glorious Apostle, faithful servant and friend of Jesus,

The name of the traitor has caused you to be forgotten by many,

But the true Church invokes you universally as the Patron of things despaired of.

Pray for me, that finally I may receive the consolations and the succor of Heaven in

all my necessities, tribulations, and sufferings, particularly (here make your request), and that I

may bless God with the Elect throughout Eternity. Amen.

God, Our Father

When your situation seems hopeless, you can always take your problems to our creator. In the Bible, God commands us to ask him for his help because he loves us. My recommendation is to pray a novena, which is a nine-day prayer.

The overall timing doesn't matter, but the prayer ought to be performed around the same time every day to establish a rhythm. Light a white candle, wait a few minutes, recite the following prayer, plead your case, then allow the candle to burn for a minimum of an hour before extinguishing it.

NOVENA TO GOD THE FATHER

God, my Heavenly Father, I adore You, and I count myself as nothing before Your Divine Majesty. You alone are Being, Life, Truth, and Goodness. Helpless and unworthy as I am, I honor You, I praise You, I thank You, and I love You in union with Jesus Christ, Your Son, our Savior and our Brother, in the merciful kindness of His Heart and through His infinite merits.

I desire to serve You, to please You, to obey You, and to love You always in union with Mary Immaculate, Mother of God and our Mother. I also desire to love and serve others for the love of You.

Heavenly Father, thank You for making me Your child in Baptism. With childlike confidence I ask You for the special favor (mention your request).

I ask that Your will may be done. Give me what You know to be the best for my soul and for the souls of those for whom I pray. Give me Your Holy Spirit to enlighten me and to guide me in the way of Your commandments and Holiness while I strive for the happiness of heaven where I hope to glorify You forever. Amen.

The Breakup Spells

First and foremost, I would like to once again implore spell-casters to defer performing breakup spells on abusive relationships. These spells cause anger and arguments and, if an abuser is provoked, they may become physically violent toward their partner.

Instead, cast send-away spells on the abuser. The second step is to encourage their partner to seek help from professional counselors of domestic violence. A great starting point is to have the victim contact the National Domestic Violence Hotline at *www.TheHotline.org*.

Animals, Insects, or Their Curios

Approach any living creature, whether it is a plant, insect, or animal, slowly. The tone of your voice must be soft and slow while your demeanor must be unassuming, as all living organisms respond favorably to these behaviors. Then respectfully introduce yourself, explain the situation, and ask them for their assistance. Act as if you were conversing with another human being who has the power to help you.

Burrowing Buddies

In the past, I frequently manifested breakup spells by simply writing the names of both people with pencil on a very small piece of paper from a brown paper bag. Then I smeared the opposite side of the paper with fresh ground meat. These papers were taken to anthills and the ants were asked to eat away at the relationships.

Later discovering that burrows are habitats for animals, I have successfully manifested breakup spells in the same fashion, offering a paper smeared with fresh food to the animal who owns the burrow. However, there are two adjustments: instead of using just ground meat, use the animal's food of choice and, the larger the animal, the larger the name paper.

Sand burrows, for instance, are usually inhabited by creatures attracted to fishy-tasting food, so the name paper would be smeared with fish meat. Below is a list of the most common burrowing animals native to Michigan, my home state, and their food of preference:

* **Groundhogs** prefer berries. Since blueberries are used in negative spellwork, I generously smear the paper with them.

* **Rats** prefer meat or cheese.

* **Snakes** prefer meat.

Cobweb Capers

Please do not use a functioning spiderweb because that poor insect went to a lot of work to build it and is actively depending on it for sustenance. Instead, use old, abandoned cobwebs.

Take a very small picture of both parties, with eyes showing, and cut out the images of their faces. Wrap each image individually in the cobweb, then wrap both images together in the remaining cobweb. As you are wrapping, state that they are trapped from interacting with each other. Then put this in a safe place, such as a box, and keep it in your possession.

Dog and Cat Catastrophes

Spell 1: Take the dirt from the foot tracks of both people and put all of it in a small brown paper bag. Add whiskers from both a black dog and a black cat. Throw it all in a fire while demanding that the two people will fight like cats and dogs.

Spell 2: Put black dog hair into the foot tracks of the man and black cat hair into the foot tracks of the woman while demanding that they will fight like cats and dogs. If both parties are of the same gender, put the dog hair into the foot track of the dominant person, such as a boss, and the cat hair into the other one.

Spell 3: Burn black dog and black cat hair to ashes. Throw the ashes in the path where the two parties will cross, while demanding that they fight.

Prisoners of Peacock Plumage

Along with Oshun, a deity of Santería who reigns over love matters, there are other deities who also reign over romance. Oshun and others favor peacocks and punish those who own the plumage, because their beloved birds have been sacrificed solely for selfish purposes.

If a person owns these feathers but is not a devotee of Oshun or other deities who favors these birds, their punishment will consist of being left without a romantic partner. Therefore, sending an anonymous gift of peacock feathers to someone who has either stolen your partner or plans to do so will result in abandonment of their romantic prospects. They will also continue to fail in future romantic affairs as long as the feathers remain in their homes.

Breakup with Bottles, Boxes, Containers, and Jars

Habanero Hatred Spell

This spell causes confusion and hatred. Obtain a bottle of habanero sauce and empty out a little of its contents in order to add other items. Put one tablespoon of poppy seeds into the bottle, then insert individual photos of both targets. Secure the cap. Keep this in your possession and shake it as often as possible while demanding that they fight.

Vexing Volcanic Ash

Mix equal amounts of volcanic ash with cayenne pepper. Then add black dog hair and black cat hair. Place name papers and/or photographs of both parties in a small jar that has a lid and transfer your mixture into the jar. Secure the lid and keep this in your possession. Shake it as often as possible while demanding that they fight.

Other Container Spells

You may also place the targets' pictures and/or name papers in a container along with either lemon juice from freshly squeezed lemons, spoiled milk, vinegar, War Water, or a mixture of two or more of these liquids. However, because these elements contain gases that could cause leakage or mini explosions, such containers must be deployed by either burying them in a path both parties will cross or in a cemetery.

Stink Box

Obtain a small box. Glue pictures of the culprit on the inside of the box lid. Smear fresh dog feces over the pictures. Place a picture or a doll of the person whom you favor inside the box, forcing that person to look at the culprit's filthy pictures. Seal the box shut.

Candle Calamity Spells

Why place pictures or petition papers underneath candles? Because it aids in manifesting the desires of the spellcaster. Here's one case that caused me to gasp in amazement.

One night, while lying on the sofa watching television and thinking that candlelight would be aesthetically pleasing, I lit a plain white candle. Being too lazy to find a coaster to protect the wood table from the heat of the candleholder, I instead used a magazine bearing the image of Pope John Paul II.

The following day, I attended church. The priest announced that a little gift shop had been launched and urged the parishioners to explore it. Upon my arrival to the shop, every attendant had this unexplainable desire to gift me, and only me, with numerous items containing images of Pope John Paul II. Politely accepting their unwanted gifts, yet baffled as to why this was occurring, I returned home with about ten different items bearing his image.

It later struck me that because a candle was set on his picture, it manifested more of the same. Thus, a lifelong lesson learned! Even a simple vigil candle spell, as described below, could manifest your desires.

Vigilante Vigil Candle

Take a long thin metal barbecue skewer, shish kebab skewer, or a long thin Phillips screwdriver and bore two holes deep into the wax of a black or white vigil candle, half an inch away from the wick, on either side. With an eyedropper or a 1 cc syringe, gently drip breakup oil into the holes, making sure not to exceed half a cc of oil into each hole or, if using an eyedropper, no more than seven drops per hole. Then lightly sprinkle cayenne pepper on the top.

Set the candle over images of the targets with the word *breakup* written over each of their foreheads. Light the candle and pray.

Candle Jar Spell for Breaking Up a Relationship

Although this spell is similar to the Candle Jar Spell for Sorrowful Idiots on pages 176-177, many ingredients in this spell are used solely for the purpose of causing arguments, confusion, and ultimately a breakup. Do not use ingredients for cursing, such as Goofer Dust, in breakup jars because they can hurt the innocent party.

Pencil

Petition paper

Breakup Oil

Pictures of the targets with eyes showing

32-ounce jar with a metal lid (without manufacturer's markings on the lid)

4 ounces War Water

4 ounces habanero sauce

4 ounces white vinegar

4 ounces spoiled milk

The juice of one freshy squeezed lemon

9 coffin nails

9 pins

9 needles

2 pica-pica pods

1 tablespoon poppy seeds

1 tablespoon red pepper flakes

1 tablespoon volcanic ash

1 charcoal briquette or disc

A generous amount of black dog hair

A generous amount of black cat hair

Broken glass

Small tube of gelled glue (e.g., Gorilla Glue, Crazy Glue)

8 black, 6-inch taper candles

Begin this spell on a Tuesday or Saturday night of a waning moon. With a pencil, inscribe the candles from top to bottom in spiral fashion with the word *breakup* for a total of nine times—and try not to lift the pencil. Anoint the candles with the oil from top to bottom. The petition paper can be crossed with the word *breakup* and anointed.

Place the pictures and the petition paper inside the jar. Put everything else except for the glue and candles in the bottle. The bottle ought to be two-thirds full. Do not fill it higher because both the vinegar and spoiled milk contain gases that can explode the jar. State your curse as many times as possible.

Before securing the lid on the jar, smear the glue on the inside lip of the lid or the threads of the jar. This is to prevent the gases from the milk and vinegar forcing the lid off. Put the lid on tightly and shake the jar vigorously.

This spell does not require a candleholder. Hold a match under the bottom of the candle until some wax has dripped onto the lid. Then firmly place the candle on the melted wax and let it harden. Check for candle stability before lighting it.

Once the candle is lit, recite your prayers and petitions aloud. This is a six-hour candle; therefore, it will help to repeat your prayers and petitions at least once more during the six-hour period. Once the candle has been consumed, remove the wax remains and throw them at a crossroad.

Repeat this spell every Tuesday and Saturday of the waning moon. Since there are normally two Tuesdays and two Saturdays a month that fall on a waning moon phase, the spell will take two months to perform.

During the waxing moon phases keep the jar in a sealed freezer bag to avoid leakage. During any day of the week, shake the jar vigorously, keeping it in the sealed bag, while screaming that these people will fight like angry cats and dogs.

When the waning moon returns, remove the jar from the bag to continue the candle work. Once the eighth candle has been consumed, smash the jar at a crossroad while again screaming your curse. Walk away and do not turn around to look back because it is a sign of distrusting the work. Do not return to that area.

Sexual Sadism

Pica-Pica Powder, also called "itching powder," is available in most botanicas or spiritual stores. It is widely used by the

Santería community to send someone away and for cursing, hexing, and breakup spells.

This spell is to prevent the culprit from engaging in sexual intercourse with your partner. Depending on the gender of your target, obtain either a black vagina or penis candle. With your soldering iron, bore a deep hole into the tip of the penis candle or into the vaginal opening of the female candle and insert Pica-Pica Powder. Then seal the hole with wax.

Inscribe the candle with the target's birth name and birth date. Next, inscribe a command, such as *uncontrollable itching*, all over the candle. Name and baptize the candle, anoint it with olive oil, and roll it in more of the powder.

Set the candle atop of either a picture of the target or a name paper along with your written command. You may either light the candle immediately or wait a few days while frequently commanding that the target's sexual organs experience ravenous itching. I will go as far as to role-play the discomfort by scratching my genitals and screaming in pain while talking to the candle.

Skull Candle Segregation

This spell has manifested great results for my breakup work and I've incorporated it into my practice ever since I had initially developed it years ago. The idea is for the innocent person to see the disgust of the other.

For this spell, you will need two skull candles: a black one to represent the predator and a white one to represent the innocent person. To understand where to bore holes into both candles, refer to the previous chapter and the section on "Preparing Your Skull Candle," which explains in detail the significance of the brain lobes as well as how to interpret the wax remains.

In bored holes of the black candle you'll place small petition papers with the command *confusion and anger* along with poppy seeds and red pepper flakes. After sealing the holes and inscribing, naming, and baptizing the candle, anoint it with olive oil, then roll it in volcanic ash. Smear the face of the candle with fresh dog feces. Set the candle over the image of the culprit.

The white candle, on the other hand, will be stuffed only with petition papers stating that the culprit is a piece of crap. So, if the culprit's name was John Doe, I would write: "John Doe is a piece of crap." After sealing the holes and inscribing, naming, and baptizing the candle, you will anoint this candle with breakup oil and set this atop the image of the innocent party.

Set the candles facing each other, forcing the white candle to stare at face of the black candle smeared with dog feces, then light them both. Every hour on the hour, go to the left side of the white candle and state aloud three times: "John Doe is a piece of crap." Go to the front of the candle and do the same, then to the right side of the candle, and, finally, to the back of its head. Once the face of the white candle has melted, there is no further need to talk to it.

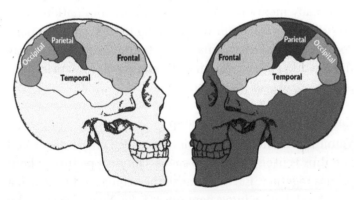

Humiliate with Human Waste

Back in the olden days, spiritual practitioners did not have a lot to work with. They creatively used whatever was available to them such as oil placed in gourds with self-made wicks instead of candles or butter and twigs to make dolls. They also successfully incorporated plants, minerals, insects, animal curios, and even human waste into their spellwork.

My mother avidly employed urine, feces, vomitus, and other personal concerns into her work. As a little girl, I thought these practices appalling. Every time I closed my eyes in disgust, her response was always the same: "If you are embarrassed or too good to get your hands dirty, then you are not the daughter of a bruja. You are just a spoiled little brat. You better find yourself a very rich man to marry when you get older because you think you're a princess!"

But after people rewarded her with gratuitous gifts for successful spell manifestation, my eyes were opened because I liked presents! Thereafter, it never bothered me again because the rewards outweighed the work involved. Here are a few spells my mother taught me.

Domination in the Workplace

As already mentioned, urine is useful in domination work. To rule over a coworker who is trying to steal your job, pour your fresh urine into a small spray bottle. Then lightly spray the coworker's workstation while stating that you're in complete control over (target's name).

Eating Away at a Relationship

Vomitus contains hydrochloric acid, which breaks down food and thus is used in breakup spells. Obtain a picture of both parties together. Eat a full meal, then squeeze the juice of a large fresh lemon into a container. Take the picture and the lemon juice to an area where the two people will cross over. Dig a hole in the ground, place the picture in the hole with the image facing you. Drink the lemon juice, then vomit on the picture. Cover this up with dirt and walk away. The HCL and acidic lemon juice will eat away at both the picture and relationship.

Soiling a Relationship

Take a small piece of brown paper bag. On one side of the paper write the name and birth date of the first party, and on the other side the second person's name and birth date. Put this in a small glass jar, then add soiled toilet water into which you had urinated and defecated. Add a charcoal briquette or disc, then take it outside and allow it to completely evaporate. Later, bury the jar in an area that both parties will cross.

Contact Magic: Laying Tricks

Ghastly Graveyard Dirt

To cause a relationship to result in a dead end, sprinkle a generous amount of graveyard dirt in the path of the two people while stating that as they step on this dirt their relationship will die. This is an especially effective spell for newlyweds.

Peonia Pangs

To cause a couple to fight, with a hammer, crush nine peonia seeds and nine peppercorns. Burn this along with nine leaves from a peanut plant. Sprinkle the ashes on the walkway, door entrance, or inside the home of the couple.

Pumpkin Paranoia

An old Palo spell is to grind nine dried pumpkin leaves along with twenty-one peppercorns into a fine powder. Peppercorns are easily breakable; just tuck them inside paper towels and pound them with a hammer, then grind them along with the leaves. Finally, sprinkle the powder on the doorstep or inside the home of the couple that you wish to separate.

Say "So Long!" with a Magical Square

Mayhem with a Magical Square

Abramelin was reputedly an Egyptian magician and teacher of the esoteric who lived centuries ago. His book exists in twelve manuscripts in which magical squares feature prominently. Each square contains words or names that relate to the magical goal of that square.

Featured in the twelfth chapter of the third manuscript of Abamelin's work is the magical square to cause quarrels and fights.

K	A	N	N	A
A	Q	A	I	
N	A	T	A	
N	I	A	Q	A
A				

Magical Squares and Two Pictures

The squares can be used in various ways, such as writing your petition on the opposite side of the paper and placing it under a candle. Another way is to place the desired square in a fireproof censer and covering it up with self-igniting powdered incense. For breakup work, my preferred method is to bind an image of both parties, with eyes showing, to the lettering of the square then bury it either in a path where both parties will cross or in a cemetery.

Sending Magical Squares

Send the happy couple a nice greeting card that is worthy of displaying or keeping. Draw the magical square either directly above, below, or opposite the message inside the card. Remember to sign someone else's name to the card.

The Sneaky Magical Square Trick

If one or both targets have either sand or dirt to their entranceway, with a stick, draw the square in the area where both are sure to step on it.

A Variety of Vengeance Spells

Falling Out of Love Water

Place name papers or pictures of the targets into a clean glass. Pour the water from your Falling Out of Love Spray bottle into the glass. Take the glass outside and let it evaporate. This takes your petition into the universe. Afterward, bury the name papers or images in a path that the two will cross.

Incense

Mix any of the breakup powders with either unscented incense or a condition incense. On a hot charcoal disc place a small petition paper commanding that the two people will break up. Put the incense over the petition paper and take it outside to burn. As both the incense and the paper burn, state your petition aloud as many times as possible.

Nature's Nasties

Imagine taking a walk in the woods or in a park on a beautiful day. The sun is shining, and the plants are glistening with dew, making their colors extraordinarily brilliant. The air is pure. The sound of birds chirping in unison is God's music, and you feel alive and at one with the universe.

You continue your gleeful walk, then Mother Nature discloses her "not so pretty" side: you are suddenly confronted with either animal feces or vomitus covered by maggots or, worse yet, a dead rotting animal being consumed by scavengers. Do you jump back in fright and gasp in disgust? I hope not!

All savvy witches know that everything nature provides, whether attractive or unappealing to the senses, is a gift. If you are performing breakup work, then you have been offered a perfect occasion to make a relationship not only end, but end in disgust.

If an animal has died, respectfully ask the spirits of both the dead animal and the live scavengers for their help. Next, insert the name papers or pictures of your targets into the matter, thank the spirits, and walk away with a big smile on your face because both a Spirit Guide and Mother Nature had gifted you with this opportunity. Then for God's sake, wash your hands!

Poignant Pastes

Grocery stores can be treasure-houses for spiritual supplies, particularly specialty stores selling items not commonly found elsewhere. Having married an Italian man, my shopping excursions frequently led me to stores catering to his ethnic group. One day, I found different types of pastes that ultimately worked very well in my breakup spells.

Obtain individual pictures, with eyes showing, of both parties. Generously apply either chili paste or anchovy paste on both images, then press them together and reinforce the bond by either completely encasing the pictures with duct tape or by stapling the edges together. The chili paste will cause arguments whereas the anchovy paste will result in mutual repulsion.

For more breakup spells, see my book *Destroying Relationships: Hoodoo Spells to Break Up, Separate, Hot Foot, and Drive off Your Foes and Rivals.*

What to Know and Do after Performing Negative Spellwork

requently, neophytes will cast spells either successfully or unsuccessfully but remain bewildered about many details such as: "Where do I put the spell's remains?" "Is there anything else that I am supposed to do?" "What if I did something wrong and the spell backfires and instead affects me?" Or the most basic, "How do I know if the spell worked?" This chapter will address these common queries and also provide you with additional information that all professional spellcasters already know, while hopefully leaving no stone unturned.

Deployment of Spell Remains

The act of *deployment*, as defined in the dictionary, is to put someone or something into use or action. Examples would include positioning military troops to engage in combat or engaging spiritual forces to assist with spellwork. It can also mean to put something into action yourself, such as placing a trick on or inside the target's clothing or in their food.

Throughout this book, you have been prompted to either bury an item, put it in a sewer, drop it in a river or stream, and take it to other venues. But why? Because once a negative spell is completed, most items such as candle wax, petition papers, containers, etc., ought not remain in your possession, nor should they be disposed of. Instead, a seasoned practitioner will ask spiritual forces to deploy or to "carry on with the spell."

What spiritual forces exist other than revered deities or your own spiritual court? Numerous ones! As we discussed earlier, they exist within animals and their curios, minerals, plants, stones, and the like. But there are also spirits living in dirt, trees, water, and even the garbage can! They exist everywhere. The key to proper deployment is to select the right means to carry out the spell and to respectfully ask for help from the spirits who dominate your selected domain.

The following are the most common deployment domains for the correlating spell purpose:

Animals and insects: Used to either eat away at something, such as a relationship, or to send away an undesired condition or person. As previously stated, explain the situation and ask for their assistance before deploying any item.

Crossroads: This is the center of where two roads cross. In the practice of Hoodoo, Santería, and other magical belief systems, it is held that there is an entity, or path of an entity, that resides at the crossroads. In Hoodoo, he is referred to as "The man at the crossroads," whereas in Santería, he is known as Eleggua, an orisha with twenty-one different paths. One of the domains he rules is the crossroads. Almost anything can be deployed at the crossroad. Sometimes Hoodoo practitioners will leave a dime as an offering of gratitude after deployment, while santeros will always leave three or twenty-one shiny pennies. Once your items have been deployed, walk away, and do not turn back or return to that area as this is a sign of disrespecting the entity by questioning his abilities.

Dirt: Dirt is usually employed in contact spells, for instance, burying a trick so that the target will come into indirect contact with it, such as crossing over or near it. Burying items in the dirt far from where the target resides or works is also employed in send-away spells to keep the target anchored down to the faraway land. The offering of gratitude is usually a dime.

Fire: Used in banishing spells, such as burning the target's business card to make the person lose their job. The offering ought to be a humble and gracious verbal expression of gratitude.

Garbage cans: Hoodoo practitioners do not place things in the garbage because of the symbolic implication that the work is garbage. However, if you practice an African Traditional Religion, such as Santería, it is believed that another path of the orisha Eleggua lives in the garbage. Although I prefer the Hoodoo methods of deployment, if the weather in Michigan is too cold for other modes, I will put the items in a brown paper bag along with three shiny pennies. Then I'll knock on the garbage can, remove the lid, and respectfully tell Eleggua the situation and ask him to carry out the spell while emphasizing that his *derecho* or offering of gratitude is inside the bag. I place the bag inside the garbage, thank him, kiss the garbage can (although that part is not necessary), replace the lid, and walk away.

Graveyards: Mostly utilized in spells that employ the spirits of deceased people or beloved animals to keep the energy of the spellwork intact. Follow all the guidelines given under "How to Acquire Graveyard Dirt" in chapter 5, but you would instead ask the spirit to keep watch over the spellwork rather than seeking graveyard dirt. Bury the item over the area of where the hand is, which is a symbolic gesture of putting the spell in the spirit's hands. If the spirit is a beloved pet, such as a dog, place the item over the area of its mouth. Remember to leave an offering of a dime as well as something that the spirit enjoyed while alive.

Rivers, sewers, or streams: These are bodies of running water used to send away an undesired condition or person. As the water runs away, so will your target or situation. Remember that lakes, oceans, or ponds are not bodies of running water. Although sewers appear to be unlikely places to speak to spirits, they nevertheless contain water, which indeed possesses a spirit, so offer a dime in gratitude for the assistance.

Trees: Usually employed to increase a spell's intensity, such as a love or cursing spell, for as the tree grows, so will the power of the spell. Talk to the tree, ask its permission to bury the items near it, and wait for feelings of consent or denial. It is said that if a leaf falls after asking the tree's permission, the answer is an unquestionable consent, especially if the leaf falls on your head. Bury the item near the tree and place a dime over it as an offering of gratitude. Cover everything with dirt and give the tree water. Although not necessary, I will also hug the tree because it not only expresses further gratitude, but it is also a grounding technique that delivers therapeutic effects.

Cleanse Your Workspace Again

Following negative spellwork, you may have attracted the curiosity of malevolent spirits. Although you have been protected from any of their malicious intents, they themselves, or their energies, might be loitering around your workroom. Don't be afraid or intimidated, just take control of the situation and get rid of them immediately. Do this by cleansing as many surfaces as possible with a formula that washes away negativity, such as Chinese Wash from chapter 2. Follow this up by pouring Florida Water into a spray bottle or filling the bottle with one teaspoon of sea salt mixed with two cups of water. Remember to avoid spraying your wood with Florida Water as it contains an alcohol base and can ruin your furniture.

Close your windows and doors, then spray around the areas while demanding or screaming: "All uninvited entities must leave my home immediately. You were not invited here, and you are not wanted here!" Immediately open a window or a door and scream: "Leave NOW!" Then slam the door shut or close the window and again spray a little more around your work area. This short ritual should eradicate their presence as they cannot remain where they had not been invited.

Ritual for Spiritual Forgiveness and Atonement

If you had properly protected yourself and your workspace during spellcasting, you will not be affected by any negative energies or repercussions emitted by the work performed, even if you did not follow the spell instructions by the letter. However, it is nevertheless prudent to ask God for his forgiveness for engaging in spiritual warfare.

Hyssop, or *Hyssopus officinalis*, is an herb of great antiquity and mentioned several times in both the Hebrew and Christian Bibles, as being a spiritual cleansing agent. It was also utilized in other countries, such as ancient Egypt, for religious purification. Hyssop is the herb to use when seeking forgiveness from God.

After performing negative spells, most Hoodoo practitioners will take baths with hyssop, drink hyssop tea, or both. Prior to bathing in it, please keep in mind that if you have open sores or wounds on your skin, including rashes, avoid any baths until you have first consulted with a physician. The same applies to allergies.

Fill your bathtub with water to your desired temperature. Then place two cups of water in a pot and place it on the stove. Turn the heat on high and once the water boils, immediately remove the pot from the stove and add a heaping tablespoon of hyssop. Allow the hyssop to steep in the water for thirteen minutes. Then strain the herbs, keeping the water and respectfully placing the herbs outside on the ground from whence they came. Drink one or two sips of the water and pour the rest into your prepared bathtub.

Remove your clothing and enter the bathtub with a printout of Psalm 51, which I lovingly refer to as "The Hyssop Psalm" because it speaks of cleansing with hyssop. While reciting this psalm aloud, try to completely immerse yourself in the water for a total of thirteen times, in between the recitation of the verses.

While performing this ritual, I highly recommend crying because it summons God's pity, and it also cleanses the soul. As the old Yiddish saying goes: "Tears are to the soul what soap is to the body."

PSALM 51 (KJV)

1 Have mercy upon me, O God, according to thy lovingkindness: according unto the multitude of thy tender mercies blot out my transgressions.

2 Wash me thoroughly from mine iniquity, and cleanse me from my sin.

3 For I acknowledge my transgressions: and my sin is ever before me.

4 Against thee, thee only, have I sinned, and done this evil in thy sight: that thou mightest be justified when thou speakest, and be clear when thou judgest.

5 Behold, I was shapen in iniquity; and in sin did my mother conceive me.

6 Behold, thou desirest truth in the inward parts: and in the hidden part thou shalt make me to know wisdom.

7 Purge me with hyssop, and I shall be clean: wash me, and I shall be whiter than snow.

8 Make me to hear joy and gladness; that the bones which thou hast broken may rejoice.

9 Hide thy face from my sins, and blot out all mine iniquities.

10 Create in me a clean heart, O God; and renew a right spirit within me.

11 Cast me not away from thy presence; and take not thy holy spirit from me.

12 Restore unto me the joy of thy salvation; and uphold me with thy free spirit.

13 Then will I teach transgressors thy ways; and sinners shall be converted unto thee.

14 Deliver me from bloodguiltiness, O God, thou God of my salvation: and my tongue shall sing aloud of thy righteousness.

15 O Lord, open thou my lips; and my mouth shall shew forth thy praise.

16 For thou desirest not sacrifice; else would I give it: thou delightest not in burnt offering.

17 The sacrifices of God are a broken spirit: a broken and a contrite heart, O God, thou wilt not despise.

18 Do good in thy good pleasure unto Zion: build thou the walls of Jerusalem.

19 Then shalt thou be pleased with the sacrifices of righteousness, with burnt offering and whole burnt offering: then shall they offer bullocks upon thine altar.

Once you have completed this ritual, leave the bathtub and blot yourself dry with a towel. Next spray yourself with Holy Water or anoint the crown of your head—and chakra points, if desired—with Blessing, Holy, or Protection Oil.

Your soul is now pure and free from any spiritual harm or consequences. The only battle that you may encounter may be feelings of guilt, especially when the spell begins to manifest. If you begin experiencing these feelings, remind yourself of the harm that the target inflicted upon you or a loved one. Thus, your spellwork was justified: "An eye for an eye, a tooth for a tooth."

How Long Will It Take for the Spell to Manifest?

This is one of the most difficult questions to answer. Sometimes spells will manifest immediately, but at other times spells may not be realized until weeks, months, or even years following the completion of the spellwork.

It is my personal belief that if manifestation has not occurred within two years, then the energy that had been produced and emitted from the spellwork will have dissipated. To avoid such disappointments, prudent spellcasters will wait for signs from the spiritual realm and intermittently check for audible, visual, or tangible movement. If signs or movement do not occur within a certain time frame, normally three months, they will perform additional spellwork to keep the energy in a constant and robust motion.

Recognize the Difference between Spiritual Signs and Selective Attention

A spiritual sign is a form of communication from an entity. It is a message that may be conveyed to you through sight, sound, touch, smell, dreams, or even through another living being. Signs are of a personal nature that are expressed through numbers (the favored mode of communication by entities), symbols, spoken words by another, names, or anything that is relevant or pertains to your spellwork. This form of communication will usually appear both randomly and unexpectedly, as opposed to your actively seeking and receiving a message.

I once performed a love spell for a client, and a week after completing the work, she persistently asked me if I had received a positive sign. As stated earlier, most professional spellcasters wait for signs from the spiritual world; they do not seek them. So she was told to have patience and faith, but she refused to listen to my advice and fervently prayed.

A few days after that last conversation with her, while driving on the expressway I saw the first name of her love interest on an exit sign. Assuming it was a subconscious form of selective attention, I ignored it. However, two days after that incident, his name appeared on a flashing neon board. It was amusing that a message was given to me on two public signs, so someone in that realm had a great sense of humor!

Once the signs were acknowledged, I thanked the spirits, told my client about the events, and never saw his name again. Her love interest returned to her about a month later.

Selective attention, on the other hand, is the process of directing our awareness to relevant stimuli while ignoring irrelevant stimuli in the environment. In other words, the human brain allows us to see or hear things that are important while filtering out unnecessary or undesired information. But that information is not lost, it is instead packed away for "a rainy day," and that's how anyone can easily confuse spiritual with physiological phenomena. The following is a hypothetical example of how selective attention can be misjudged as a spiritual sign.

While happily dating a man named David, I had to drive the same work-related ten-mile route every day for a week, while never noticing that one of the streets is named "David." My brain knows about the street name, but for my conscious thoughts, it was an irrelevant stimulus. However, because the brain is a complex, relatively autonomous piece of machinery, it makes the decision to store that information somewhere in my subconscious.

Six months later, David leaves me, so I cast a spell on him to return. Then my boss directs me to drive that old ten-mile route that I had driven while having been in a happy relationship. While on that path, I look up and see a street sign that says "David" and think to myself: "Oh my God, it's a spiritual sign!" Well, no it is not. My brain had already processed that street name six months ago and has brought it to my attention because that stimulus is now relevant to me. But had I not known about this phenomenon, I would have been convinced, beyond a shadow of a doubt, that is was a spiritual sign.

Many times clients will tell me that spiritual signs pop up on their computer screens such as website banners or emojis. In most cases, that information had always been there, but at the time they had interacted with the events, it was irrelevant stimuli. In other cases, people will actively seek signs while subconsciously knowing they will find them.

Almost all seasoned spellcasters know about selective attention and thus the reason that we do not seek spiritual signs but instead await them. Often movement, or even manifestation, will occur without spiritual signs. So do not be discouraged if it doesn't happen.

Recognizing Movement in Spellwork

With regard to spellwork, *movement* can be defined as an obvious change in a person's attitude or actions that complement the spellcaster's desires. There will be recognizable indicators such as variations—or even deviations if the target is the recipient of negative spellwork—in gestures, behaviors, or verbal expressions. Additionally, spellcasters can even gauge inanimate objects for movement, such as the breakdown of important machines or cars.

The following are just a few examples of movement in spellwork:

* Breakup spells may cause arguments or avoidance between the targets.

* Cursing and hexing spells usually cause the target to become anxious or fearful.

* Send-away spells will provoke a person to entertain the idea of seeking employment or housing elsewhere.

Movement is a temporary condition and does not guarantee successful spell manifestation. Therefore, this becomes a crucial time to perform additional spellwork to fully realize your desires. Think of it this way: Movement can be compared to the target hanging on the edge of a cliff. Additional spellwork is akin to having your foot giving that culprit the final kick!

Indicators of Successful Spell Manifestation

There are several indicators of successful spell manifestation. Some are subjective, based on the target's feelings, while others are objective, or blatantly obvious.

Such objective indicators of successful manifestation include breakup spells when people have severed their relationships, send-away spells when the target has permanently fled, or binding spells that render the target permanently incapable of causing further harm to you or others.

Cursing spells, on the other hand, may manifest in a multitude of various scenarios. One never really knows what our spiritual court considers justified revenge and may take the matter into their own hands to determine what they consider the appropriate punishment.

The following are some of the most common indicators of successful manifestation:

* **Accidents:** Either a life-threatening or debilitating calamity could be suspicious and an indication of a curse. However, a string of smaller accidents is usually the norm and will make the target think, "Someone is out to get me."

* **Avoidance:** People, usually more than one, will suddenly begin to sidestep or shun the target. Or the target will avoid others.

* **Apathy:** People are suddenly unemotional toward the target's misfortunes.

* **Appliance breakdowns:** Several appliances cease to work in a short period of time, or electrical malfunctions occur.

* **Bad luck:** The target has an ongoing run of bad luck.

* **Dismissal:** People no longer value the target's input or opinions.

* **Difficulty sleeping:** A sudden onset, lacking precipitating causes, such as stress, anxiety, or having problem-solving decisions to make. Nightmares are often associated.

* **Emotional variances:** Undesirable feelings, lacking rational reasons for the sensations such as depression, anxiety, fear, restlessness, or even feelings of impending doom.

* **Fatigue:** There is an alteration in their normal daily activities caused by physiological interruptions and the need to rest or sleep. Sometimes, exhaustion is present with undue cause.

* **Female facial hair:** Sudden hormonal imbalances are often associated with curses.

* **Financial difficulties:** There can be sudden, and ongoing, financial losses with the inability to recuperate or recover from the damage.

* **Fires:** Often caused by a practitioner working with an entity who rules this domain.

* **Floods:** This is usually the result of one of two factors. Sometimes a practitioner will have worked with an entity who rules the domain of water. However, I have often seen a practitioner working with an entity who rules the domain of fire, but the spell was either unjustified or went awry. Then another entity will step in to protect the target and prevent a potential fire by flooding the area that would have been attacked.

* **Gynecomastia:** A sudden increase in the amount of breast gland tissue in men.

* **Health problems:** Usually deteriorating in nature while physicians are unable identify the cause or diagnose the illness. Yet, at other times, there may be a sudden onset

of a devastating health crisis, such as cancer or cardio-vascular insults.

* **Isolation:** People become less visible or outspoken.

* **Jewelry:** Protective amulets or jewelry will "take the hit," meaning that they will shield the target from the curse and take it upon themselves. Then the jewelry breaks from enduring the negative energy and tension. If this occurs, further spellwork is indicated as the jewelry protected the target.

* **Pets become ill:** As with protective jewelry, pets will also "take the hit" for their owner. Further spellwork is indicated as the pet protected the target.

* **Profuse sweating:** An indicator of psychological or physiological stress.

* **Silver turning black:** A diagnostic tool that many rootworkers turn to in ascertaining if a curse has been placed on a client is the use of silver. A silver object is placed inside the client's mouth, and if the object turns black, it is a definitive indication that the client is cursed.

* **Weight gain or severe weight loss:** An indication that the target is experiencing either anxiety, depression, or both. It's one of the first signs to look for.

Last, but certainly not least, a common occurrence is that someone (or even the target) tells you about the target's misfortune. It is my humble opinion that a member of one's spiritual court prompts another to do so.

Do you recall, in chapter 1, the story of my horrible neighbor Abbey? After having placed a few spells cursing that woman, nothing seemed to work, as if Satan was her Guardian Angel. But I didn't give up because, unless she's a Holy Entity or my spells were not justified, something had to give! After two years of perpetually placing cursing spells on her, one day she approached me out of the clear blue sky, in a humble and submissive manner, just to inform me that she had cancer.

While saying "I'm so sorry to hear this," I was instead thinking to myself: "My work finally manifested!" But, as previously stated, one never knows how a curse will manifest. I did not ask for this disease; instead, my desire was for her to receive a deserving punishment. Obviously, my spiritual court decided that cancer was the justified penalty.

She never bothered me again. Thus, another lesson learned in perseverance.

Expressing Gratitude to Your Spiritual Court

Once a spell has manifested, it is important to remain humble. I will not allow or accept direct verbal gratitude from my clients for favorable outcomes as I am merely an instrument. All expressions of gratitude must instead be relayed directly from my clients to my spiritual court, via speaker phone while I sit near my altar.

Then I personally place a lit white vigil candle, fresh white carnations in a vase, and a fresh glass of cold drinking water on my altar or small wood table. Finally, I humbly and passionately express aloud gratitude for their assistance.

These little gestures go a long way because if their assistance is needed for future spellwork, my spiritual court knows that my soul is humble, and they will certainly help me again. Remember to refresh the water daily because nobody likes stale water. After the candle has been completely consumed, remove the items from the altar and, once again, express gratitude verbally.

What If the Target's Punishment Is Too Harsh?

Being empathetic to someone's hardships is an honorable attribute and obviously a result of being a good person with a loving soul. However, it is neither prudent nor wise to feel guilt or remorse if the target is suffering from your spiritual retribution.

When your spells begin to manifest, the target will suffer hardships, but I implore you to please always remember what first prompted you to cast your spells. Also try to remember that a leopard rarely changes its spots.

I learned this lesson the hard way from my past mistakes, and I've made quite a few in my lifetime. Well, actually not a just few but, in all honesty, I've made so many that I could probably write an entire encyclopedia entitled "The Bloopers and Blunders that Miss Aida Has Made with Spellwork"! However, we learn from our mistakes as they are the stepping-stones toward wisdom.

Nevertheless, I once made a four-in-one mistake after having felt guilt and remorse when my negative spellwork manifested. But I later realized that it happened as both a learning as well as a teaching event because this story has been shared in the past with hundreds of appreciative people—and will now be relayed to you.

My Four-in-One Mistake

Dora was the president of a small organization and one of the nastiest people you would ever want to meet. She was a liar and a predator who would manipulate, hurt people, and create chaos for no apparent reason other than, as she had once stated, "I like to sit back and watch the show." No matter how many people were hurt, she always seemed to walk away from the incidents free from accountability.

Although she did nothing to me, she created devastation in the lives of good people. The last straw that broke this camel's back was when she caused an accountant to lose her job simply because Dora was jealous of her new car.

So I performed a mirror box spell, generously wrapped it in duct tape, and placed it in the freezer. As you now know, mirror box spells will not only prevent the target from harming others—as will freezer spells—but their energies will bounce right back to them. Following that event, Dora's luck began to change for the worse, and everything that could possibly go wrong in her life did! She became anxious and fearful. Not knowing that I was the cause of her misfortune, she turned to me in a state of desperation for spiritual help.

She had contacted me around twenty times, crying like a baby, while hysterically relaying every single devastating event she had encountered. Her demeanor changed from that of a grown evil woman to a victimized little girl, and it broke my heart.

Feeling guilt and remorse for my actions, I made the decision to disassemble the mirror box spell. My mother, a seasoned practitioner, pleaded with me not to do it. But I arrogantly viewed my mother as just an old woman who didn't understand that Dora had changed for the better. As I started to take it apart, my mother stood right next to me saying: "You'll be sorry, STUPIDA!"

After detaching all of the duct tape, I removed one of the six mirror tiles, and that event was like a scene from a horror movie. The energy released from the box was so forceful and evil that it made me stumble. Thank God it was disassembled outdoors; otherwise that energy would have been confined inside my home. Days later, Dora regained her strength and was once again the nasty person she had always been. Only this time her wicked shenanigans were amplified.

Unfortunately, once a spell is disassembled, it becomes more difficult to achieve a future successful manifestation on the same person. This is because your spiritual court will most likely believe that your attitude toward the target is frivolous, and they will not take you seriously. They will often ignore your requests for further help with the same target, even if it's a different spell.

Now, a review of what not to do if you have second thoughts about your spellwork:

1. Don't feel sorry for the target.
2. Don't ignore a spiritual elder's advice.
3. Don't disassemble a spell or remove its power.
4. Don't make your spiritual court doubt you.

Exception to the Rule: The Doll

There is one exception to the rule of eluding spellwork reversal, and that is what to do with your doll once the work has manifested. Unless you plan to keep it awhile as an insurance policy in the event that the target decides to bother you again, the life essence within the doll must be removed.

You don't want to keep a doll in your possession forever, do you? Also, you certainly don't want to cause death to a person through the doll because, as stated before, if you're reading this book, you are obviously alive and therefore a death spell is not justified revenge.

Fill a bucket halfway with ammonia. Hold the doll in both hands and stare into its face while loudly proclaiming: "By my God-given powers, I remove the life essence of (target's name) from this doll. Begone!" Immediately immerse the doll in the ammonia and keep it in the bucket for at least twenty minutes. Then throw the doll in the garbage.

Why Didn't the Spell Manifest?

Sometimes spellwork will not manifest for reasons caused by actions of the spellcasters, their clients, or by spiritual intervention. The following are the most common causes.

Casting Doubt

Questioning the efficacy of the spells or being impatient with the timing of their manifestation is in fact lacking confidence in, or doubting, the spellwork. These behaviors act as a metaphorical vacuum cleaner, suctioning back all the energies emitted into the universe directed toward the target. In other words, it draws them right back to the starting point. Then the energies will either become severely weakened or will dissipate.

Additionally, if spiritual assistance was utilized in the work, these behaviors are a direct insult to the entities because you have cast doubt on their abilities. As a result, it may immediately alienate their willingness to assist in spell manifestation.

Even if one hires a seasoned spellcaster to perform the spellwork, the behaviors of the client directly affect the spells in the same manner. Thus, when clients continue to question the spellwork, the practitioners will usually become irritated because they know these behaviors will affect their spells inappropriately.

Obviously, the practitioner ought to show their clients, by photograph or video, how the spell was assembled and what was used because, after all, their clients have the right to see how their monies were utilized. However, once the spell has been completed, it is prudent to patiently await spell manifestation.

Interference with a Target's Karma

The target may be destined to accomplish something specific in this lifetime, and the spellwork may interfere with that fate. Perhaps the target was destined to be punished in a different way by a different person or entity or maybe perform something noble in the future? Only spirit knows!

A clear example of that is Abraham Lincoln. When he was elected president of the United States, hundreds of cursing effigies were made in an effort to kill him. However, it was his karma to first provide freedom from slavery, which took spiritual precedence. Then after he effectively did so, his death shortly followed. It appears that the effigies indeed worked after the purpose of his destiny was fulfilled.

Spiritual Protection

The target may be wearing amulets, charms, crystals, herbs, minerals, oils, or washes all designed for spiritual protection. However, unless the target is wearing protection 24/7, there may be a window of opportunity when the protection is removed, depending upon the type of soul the person possesses. If that soul is negatively tainted, in most cases, members of your spiritual court will find that window and take appropriate action for the sake of righteousness. Nonetheless, it is my profound belief that no amulet, charm, crystal, entity, etc., is stronger than God and, if one appeals to him for justice, he will avenge you.

Unjustified Spellwork

As discussed in chapter 1, the punishment must be proportionate to the crime; otherwise karmic paybacks can be harsh. But if your spiritual court understands that you erroneously, but sincerely, believed that negative spellwork was justified, nobody will be affected. In other words, the spells will be null and void.

Weak Spell, Strong Aura

If the target has a healthy and radiant aura, it will easily ward off minute undesirable forces. It is my personal belief that when an evil person intentionally inflicts harm on another, it makes him or her happy. That happiness, in turn, nurtures the aura, thus making it stronger.

However, the aura can be weakened by consecutive spells. Once negative spellwork has been implemented on a person with a radiant aura, it will still affect the aura even if causing minimal damage. If you are persistent, your work will wear down the aura, eventually causing the tears and holes leaving the target vulnerable to harm.

Think of it as throwing stones against a plastic sheet covering and protecting a carpet. The first few stones will cause dents. If you continue to throw stones at it, it will tear, and if you throw more stones, it will ultimately produce holes in the plastic sheet. Now, you can damage the carpet however you wish.

This is the main reason I categorically stress the importance of perseverance in spellwork. Don't just perform a onetime spell or a spell involving minimal effort, then later surrender to a false self-proclamation that the spell didn't work. Instead recognize what you are doing, how it is affecting your target, and implement further spellwork.

And Just When You Think the Spell Didn't Work ... VOILA!

The occasion may arrive when you feel enough time and energy have been invested on your target and you're tired. That's fine because exhaustion implies that a heck of a lot of your energy has been produced toward manifestation—which is a good thing.

Although easier said than done, try to forget about the spellwork because obsession may draw back the energies. Have faith the spell will manifest, your spiritual court is handling it accordingly, and results will be realized at the appropriate time.

If it appears that nothing is working, do not dispose of any objects that are in your possession. Many times, I had completely forgotten about spellwork, then later find items, such as in my freezer, and think to myself, "It didn't work." But I still kept the items right where they were. Eventually, all the spells manifested.

Sometimes, spells take longer to manifest for specific reasons only known to Spirit. I once performed a spell on a politician, but only because he was interfering with my personal life. A year later, I saw one of the spell objects and honestly believed the spell was a failure, but again, I left the object alone. Two months after that, he ended up in prison for extorting a million dollars from a hospital. So Spirit was killing three birds with one stone: expose him, punish him, and, of lesser importance, getting him out of Miss Aida's life!

So just when you think it didn't work, have faith because, most often than not, it will. Just understand that there's a reason for everything and something of greater importance may take precedence. Have patience!

CONCLUSION

Once again, the sentimental phase of book writing has arrived. For me, it is always a bittersweet time. The bitterness arises from having had you join me on an exciting journey through many of my life events, then having to say good-bye. Yet, I feel delight because you have given this old woman an opportunity to share many insights with you, including the intricacies of effective magical practices, people's appropriate as well as inappropriate behaviors, spirituality, self-behavioral modifications, and most importantly, prayers, potions, and more than one hundred successful spell recipes! Hopefully, you will have gained a vast amount of knowledge based on my triumphant experiences as well as my failures.

There's an old African proverb: "When a knowledgeable old person dies, a whole library disappears." If only I had heeded the contents of this priceless proverb when I was younger and paid more attention to my family's teachings, I would have been a more knowledgeable practitioner. Sadly, youth is wasted on the young who don't listen until it's too late. However, now that I am older, it is my duty to share as much as I know, as did my elders, to the succeeding generations.

The most important lesson I wish for you to remember is to go back to the beginning of this book and read about how my Godmother's will both directly and negatively affected a powerful babalawo's life. Why was she successful? Because she possessed all the necessary qualities needed for successful spell manifestation: determination, patience, persistence, and self-confidence. If you've got those qualities under your belt, then you've got what it takes!

Allow me to express my gratitude to you for joining me on this adventure. Thank you!

I am available for presentations. You can find me on my website MissAida.com.

Also feel free to join me on Facebook: Facebook.com/MissAidaPsychic.

BIBLIOGRAPHY

Aida, Miss. *Cursing and Crossing: Hoodoo Spells to Torment, Jinx, and Take Revenge on Your Enemies.* Forestville, California: Lucky Mojo Curio Company, 2017.

———. *Destroying Relationships: Hoodoo Spells to Break Up, Separate, Hot Foot, and Drive off Your Foes and Rivals.* Forestville, California: Lucky Mojo Curio Company, 2018.

———. *Hoodoo Cleansing and Protection Magic: Banish Negative Energies and Ward Off Unpleasant People.* Newburyport, Massachusetts: Weiser Books, 2020.

———. *MissAida.com.*

Aligheri, Dante. *The Inferno.* Barnes & Noble Classic Series, Dover Publications, 2003.

"Anatomy of the Brain." *MayfieldClinic.com.*

"The Apostle's Creed." *AnglicanOnline.org.*

BibleGateway.com.

Burton, Neel, M.D. "The Psychology of Scapegoating." *PsychologyToday.com.*

Canizares, Raul. *Helping Yourself With Selected Prayers,* Volume 2. Old Bethpage, New York: Original Publications, 2004.

"Characteristics of a Sociopath." *HealthGuidance.org.*

Cunningham, Scott. *Cunningham's Encyclopedia of Magical Herbs.* Woodbury, Minnesota: Llewellyn Publications, 2009.

Dennis, Rabbi Geoffrey W. *Encyclopedia of Jewish Myth, Magic, and Mysticism.* Woodbury, Minnesota: Llewellyn Publications, 2016.

Elworthy, Frederick Thomas. *The Evil Eye: The Classic Account of an Ancient Superstition.* Mineola, New York. Dover Publications, 2004.

Fenton, Sasha. *Tea Cup Reading: A Quick and Easy Guide to Tasseography.* York Beach, Maine: Red Wheel/ Weiser, LLC, 2002

Gager, John G. *Curse Tablets and Binding Spells from the Ancient World.* New York: Oxford University Press, 1992.

The Holy Bible, King James Version, Rev. Edition, Thomas Nelson, Inc. 1976.

"How To Tell If Your Friend Is Trying To Steal Your Friends With 6 Red Flags." *EliteDaily.com.*

Hurston, Zora Neale. *Mules And Men.* J. B. Lipponcott, 1935. Reprinted New York: Harper Collins, 1990.

Illes, Judika. *Encyclopedia of Mystics, Saints & Sages: A Guide to Asking for Protection, Wealth, Happiness, and Everything Else!* New York: HarperOne Publications, 2011.

Kertzer, Rabbi Morris N. *What is A Jew?* New York: Touchstone Publications, 1996.

Kim, Jean. M.D. "Why He Hits: The Psychology of an Abuser." *PsychologyToday.com.*

Laremy, Robert. *The Psalm Workbook.* Old Bethpage, New York: Original Publications, 2001.

Morgan, Michael A., trans. *Sepher Ha-Razim: The Book of The Mysteries.* Chico, California: Scholars Press, 1983.

"Narcissistic Personality Disorder." *MayoClinic.org.*

The National Domestic Violence Hotline. *TheHotline.Org.*

New Health Advisor. "Does Marijuana Count As a Depressant?" *HealthAdvisor.org.*

"Nikola Tesla: The Secret Behind Numbers 3, 6, and 9." *InfinityExplorers.com.*

Pajeon, Kala & Ketz. *The Candle Magick Workbook*. New York: Kensington Publishing Corporation, 1991.

"Pareidolia: Seeing Faces in Unusual Places." *LiveScience.com*.

"Prayers to Saint Joan of Arc." *DailyPrayers.org*.

"Probable Occasion When Each Psalm was Composed." *BlueLetterBible.org*.

Puckett, Newbell Niles, PhD. *Folk Beliefs of The Southern Negro*. Raleigh, N.C.: The University of North Carolina Press, 1926.

"Routine Hair Shedding: Why it Happens and How Much to Expect." *HealthLine.com*.

"Self Esteem and Effective Communication Skills." *Healthfully.com*.

"7 Signs Someone is Trying to Steal Your Partner." *PowerOfPositivity.com*.

"16 Signs That Your Coworker is Undermining You." *BusinessInsider.com*.

"Touch DNA Analysis: Using the Literature to Help Answer Some Common Questions." *ForensicMag.com*.

"20 Inspirational Quotes on Simplicity." *HabitsForWellbeing.com*.

"23 Nikola Tesla Quotes to Become the Inventor of Your Dreams." *Goalcast.com*.

Tzu, Sun. *The Art Of War*. (5th century BCE). Public domain.

"Why Do We Love to Gossip?" *PsychologyToday.com*.

Yronwode, Catherine. *Hoodoo Herb and Root Magic: A Materia Magica of African-American Conjure*. Forestville, California: Lucky Mojo Curio Company, 2002.

ABOUT THE AUTHOR

Born into a Cuban family who practiced Santeria, Palo, and Brujeria, **MISS AIDA** is a natural-born medium, Santeria initiate, Hoodoo practitioner, and author. She is also a registered nurse and a United States Air Force veteran. A renowned authority on Hoodoo, she is available for workshops. Visit her at *www.missaida.com*.